D1233390

# A Way Home

# A Way Home

## THE BAPTISTS TELL THEIR STORY

Edited by
James Saxon Childers

TUPPER AND LOVE
ATLANTA

HOLT · RINEHART · WINSTON
NEW YORK · CHICAGO · SAN FRANCISCO

Published simultaneously in Canada by Holt, Rinehart
and Winston of Canada, Limited.

Library of Congress Catalog Card Number: 64-15304

First Edition

Designer: Ernst Reichl
81394-0114
Printed in the United States of America

# Foreword

I live out in the country and on weekends students from the colleges and universities nearby come out, and sometimes young married couples. We were talking, one afternoon, about religion and I heard a girl ask: "Well, why *are* you a Baptist?"

Some of the others heard, too, and we listened. The young fellow was a postgraduate student who had learned all he could about engineering; but when she asked him why he was a Baptist, he hesitated and then said: "Well, you see my folks were Baptists. I was brought up in a Baptist home."

After the young people left, some of us who are older kept talking about churches and about how many people know why they belong to one church rather than to another; and how many—like the young fellow—just inherited a church. A few days later I stopped in a bookstore and asked for something about the Baptists. I wanted a book that would tell, briefly and in an interesting way, something about their history, about what they do in community service, and about what they believe. The man said he did not have all that in one book.

My partner and I, as publishers, believed there was a need for such a book. About one-third of the Protestants in the

United States are Baptists and many of them are not aware of their history. Many are not quite sure of just what Baptists believe. Some have no idea of the work being done today by Baptists in homes for children, in hospitals, in homes for the aged, in education.

It is intended that readers of this book shall gain a knowledge of Baptist churches and an understanding of Baptist beliefs. It is intended, too, that they shall gain a realization of what Baptists are doing in the world at present, and a whole understanding of the denomination.

The book has been planned with the help, and constant advice, of a number of Baptist leaders. There are chapters from statesmen, pastors, educators, administrators, and officers of various Baptist organizations. All are authorities on Baptist work and each directly discusses the activity that concerns him most. In the midst of their many obligations, they have given time, and thought, and work because they believed that the Baptist story, with its facts and fascinating side lights, needed to be told in this new and interesting way. They have written both for Baptists themselves and for any others who might become interested in the Baptists, in what they believe and what they stand for.

Because of book length we have had to limit some of the authors—for instance, Dr. James L. Sullivan could not possibly tell the vast story of the Sunday School Board of the Southern Baptist Convention in the pages allotted to him, so with characteristic friendliness he gave up telling of their huge publication program and all their other multiple undertakings and limited himself to the subject "Religious Education in Baptist Churches." Just so, Dr. Glenn H. Asquith, of the American Baptist Convention, told only of their publications and did not discuss their church educational program and their many other activities.

The remarkable story of the Baptists is presented here—their history, their basic beliefs, their accomplishments. We are indebted to these men for telling the story in such an informative and interesting way.

—J. S. C.

# CONTENTS

*THE BEGINNINGS OF THE BAPTIST STORY—THEIR HISTORY* 1

A New Voice in Europe: The Baptists Speak Out 3
The Baptists and the Making of the American Colonies 11
Frontier Days—and the Baptists Push On 29
1845: The Division 40
Historical Consultants
Robert A. Baker
and
Robert G. Torbet

*THE BAPTIST STORY TODAY—THEIR WORKS AND THEIR WAYS* 49

The Training of Their Ministers 51
Sydnor L. Stealey

Their Home Missions 62
Courts Redford

Their Foreign Missions 70
John E. Skoglund

Religious Education in Baptist Churches 83
James L. Sullivan

The Christian Campus 91
Andrew B. Martin

Their Publications 98
Glenn H. Asquith

They Care When You Are a Child 106
W. R. Wagoner

They Tend the Sick 118
T. Sloane Guy, Jr.

They Look After You When Age Comes 128
Gerald I. Gingrich

*TELL ME WHAT THEY SAY* 137

I Go to Church on Sunday 139
Raymond L. Guffin, Jr.

Hear the Baptists Singing 144
Walter Hines Sims

My Church and My State 152
Harold Stassen

On My Baptist Faith 160
Brooks Hays

I Have Been a Baptist All My Life 165
Benjamin E. Mays

*TELL ME THEIR BELIEFS* 173

What Makes a Baptist a Baptist? 175
Josef Nordenhaug

Inside a Baptist Church 186
Theodore F. Adams

*THERE IS NO END TO THE STORY* 199
R. Dean Goodwin

************

APPENDIX 205
*Did You Know* This *About the Baptists?* 207
C. E. Bryant

# A Way Home

# THE BEGINNINGS OF THE BAPTIST STORY— THEIR HISTORY

*HISTORICAL CONSULTANTS—*

Robert A. Baker
Professor of Church History
Southwestern Baptist Theological Seminary

Robert G. Torbet
Dean and Professor of Church History
Central Baptist Theological Seminary

# A New Voice in Europe: The Baptists Speak Out

There is a small book, about four inches by six, in the great library at Oxford University in England, and its pages are yellowed by the three-and-a-half centuries since it was published in 1612. It has one of those curious and unwieldy titles that they used back at the time of the first Queen Elizabeth and during the reign of the wizened little man who came after her, King James I. The title is *A Short Description of the Mistery of Iniquity*, and the battered little book should have a great meaning to Baptists because both the book and the man who wrote it play an important part in Baptist beginnings.

There are only four copies of the book known to us now, and it is surprising that there are this many because James had sent his men about London and wherever else the book could be found to destroy it. The strangest fact of all is how one particular copy escaped. It is the copy in the library at Oxford, and, if you are properly introduced and vouched for, you can go there and see the book and handle it. For any man there is a curious sense of nearness and reality, and for a Baptist there could be an upsurge of the spirit as he opens the book and reads its everlasting inscription.

Thomas Helwys wrote the book at a time when men bent the knee and spoke of the "divine right of kings." To question the power of church or rule of king was to risk prison and death; but Helwys had the backing of the scriptures and a courage from God, and the rights that he proclaimed were the rights of the common man. He denied that kings had divine authority over the souls of men or could in any way shape their worship. Helwys, the founder of the first Baptist church in England, ignored all threat to his personal liberty, and even risk of his life, so that he might proclaim the freedom of his soul and the same freedom for every man. He took a copy of his book—it is the copy that is in the library at Oxford now—and he wrote an inscription on the flyleaf. Then he put on his hat and cloak and set out to see the king, to take him the book. The inscription read:

> Heare o King, and dispise not ye counsell of ye poor, and let their complaints come before thee.
>
> The king is mortall man and not God, therefore hath no power over ye immortall souls of his subjects, to make laws and ordinances for them, and to set spiritual Lords over them . . .

This is the inscription that Helwys wrote, and, in the writing, he penned his own prison sentence and his death warrant. The king ordered him sent to prison, and this is the last we know of him. There is no record of what happened to him after that.

Some years before *The Mistery of Iniquity* was written, or even thought of, a sick man came one day to Broxtowe Hall, the prosperous and happy home of Thomas and Jane Helwys. They took the sick man in, made him welcome and comfortable, and gave him the best room and the best care. The man, John Smyth, was a learned man with a questioning mind, concerned primarily with things spiritual. He was an ordained minister of the Church of England and had preached in the city of Lincoln in 1600; but the people there had found a tinge of nonconformity in his preaching and they had turned him out. He packed his things and left, heading out on more than an ordinary journey. He went first to the home of his friend, Thomas Helwys, and through the long weeks of convalescence the two men sat by the fire and talked.

There are many persons and many factors in the beginning of the Baptists, but certainly these two men, sitting late by the crusted and glowing fire, seeking answers to their questions, are a fascinating part of the story. They were both members of the Church of England, but like many men in the Anglican Church at this time of spiritual restlessness and discontent they were questioning the dogma and authority of the church, wondering about its structure and its meaning, and were turning from it to search the scriptures for themselves and find their own answers.

It had been only about seventy-five years before this time that Henry VIII, in 1534, for reasons both political and personal and with no trace of spiritual intent, had broken with the Holy Roman church and had taken England completely out of Rome's orbit. It was then that Henry, with no authority except his own, had declared himself head of both church and state, and by his personal will and signature had established the Church of England, proclaiming that the religion of the throne must be the religion of the people. Now in England church and state were one. Now the conscience of the people rested on the whim of a king.

Throughout the rest of the sixteenth century, through the long reign of the first Queen Elizabeth until she died in 1603, and then on into the time of James I, the throne declared the faith of the people and decreed the form of their worship. Some of the people, though, were beginning to ask questions, and to say that a king does not decide the worship of a people or tell any man how he shall pray. They were even beginning to challenge the Anglican church and to doubt its precepts and power. Throughout the kingdom there was a growing dissent, and two of the men who were troubled were John Smyth and Thomas Helwys.

At the time that Smyth first came to Helwys' home he was already a member of one of the challenging groups, the Puritans, but he was debating an even more drastic move: that of becoming a Separatist. The Puritans took the stand that they were willing to accept the Church of England, both in its form and authority, but they wanted to purify it from every possible trace of the Church of Rome. The Separatists, on the other hand, were going much further in their dissent from the Anglican church. They were saying that the Church of England had been established by the state, in the person of the king, but the way to realize the true church was by congregations separate from the state, and with each congregation bound together by its own covenant. It was, therefore, right for the congregations to separate themselves from any trace of state authority, and for each man within the congregation to read his own Bible for himself and preach God's Word as he found it in the scriptures. Such teaching as this could, of course, undermine both church and state, seriously lessening the power of the throne, and James quickly admonished his forces to suppress it.

Through the ages the great spiritual understandings of men have always grown out of other beliefs and teachings, and Smyth and Helwys did not suddenly break from the church in which they had been reared. They did not sit by the fire and create a great faith out of nothing. They wrestled with the beliefs and the teachings of other men, and with the dogma of the church in which one was a member and the other a minister, and they endlessly searched the scriptures. It was in the sufferings of their souls that their beliefs grew, and their faith was decided, and they knew that they must separate from the Church of England and find a new way.

In telling this story of Baptist beginnings we have particularly told the story of two men, Smyth and Helwys. There is a reason for this. In the first place we know a good deal about these men; but the most important reason is that John Smyth became the leader of a group in Holland that was to be the first Baptist congregation. Indeed, it has been said of Smyth that he was the "founder of the modern Baptist churches." And Thomas Helwys, as we have told you, founded the first of the Baptist churches in England.

At this time all men who did not adhere strictly to the teachings and practices of the Church of England were called Nonconformists, and King James in anger at them and in fear of their teachings had said: "I will make them conform or I will harry them out of the land." This plan of persecution he followed, either forcing them to leave the country or putting them in prison.

Smyth and Helwys decided to leave England in 1608 for Amsterdam, going there because of the religious liberty then being extended to anyone in Holland. Other Separatists had already gone from England to Amsterdam, and these people were forming themselves into various groups for worship according to their individual beliefs. (One of these groups founded the Pilgrim church in Amsterdam and it was members of this church who sailed in 1620—"the Pilgrim fathers"—on the *Mayflower* for New England.)

The group that formed around John Smyth as their leader were some thirty-seven men and women. They came together because their beliefs embodied most of the Baptist principles that have continued through the years and are now essential parts of the Baptist faith. Because of their decision on these principles, their announcement of them, and their dedication to them, this congregation that was formed in Amsterdam, Holland, in about the year 1609, with their clear Baptist point of view, is now recognized as the first Baptist congregation in the modern world.

Among their beliefs they insisted that a church is properly made up only of those who have responded in their own faith to the teachings of the Gospel, and have given witness of their faith in believer's baptism.

They called for church freedom from any dictate of king or state, the absolute separation of church and state.

They pronounced the dignity of every human being and the liberty of every human soul, declaring that each soul can, and must, choose for itself alone in the realm of the spirit.

They said there could be no force to compel men to hold any particular position of faith, and it was Thomas Helwys who wrote the first English words that set forth man's right to total freedom in worship, no matter what the form of his worship might be: "Let them be heretics, Turks, Jews, or whatsoever, it appertains not to the earthly power to punish them in the least measure." These words of complete religious freedom ring down through the years and echo clearly in our own Constitution and in the constitution of every democracy.

This was the New Voice in Europe. These were the beliefs of the people who later were called Baptists. This was the borning of a new faith, the beginning of a new freedom, the first steps of millions and millions of men, of all the Baptists who have come after.

The people of Smyth's congregation continued their worship until slowly, in the exercise of their individual religious liberty, they began to find differences of opinion among themselves, particularly in regard to church authority concerning baptism. The differences grew until Smyth and Helwys, in great personal sorrow, ended their relationship in about the year 1611. Smyth remained in Holland, and Helwys, knowing the risk he ran, led some eight or ten men and women back to England. There he founded the first Baptist church on English soil, the congregation worshiping secretly at Spitalfield, just outside the walls of London.

For probably a year they continued their secret worship, but Helwys, a man of total conviction and courage, said that men should not have to hide their worship of God and that he was coming out into the open to tell his faith to all men, including the king. So he took a copy of his book—which may have been published in Holland—and he wrote with a brave and steady hand: "Heare o King . . ." He wrote slowly, knowing that prison and death might be his answer, but he wrote without faltering: "The king is mortall man and not God, therefore hath no power over ye immortall souls of his subjects . . ."

When he finished his writing he put on his hat and cloak and carrying his book, his declaration of the soul freedom of every man, he set out to see the king.

He himself was seen no more, but his work was done. The tradition of the Baptists in England was already under way, and as Henry C. Vedder, one of the greatest of all Baptist historians, has said: "After 1610 we have an unbroken succession of Baptist churches." He pointed out that there is unquestionable documentary evidence to prove this succession, and he added that "from about the year 1641, at the latest, Baptist doctrine and practice have been the same in all essential features that they are today."

With the disappearance of Helwys, but with the Baptists clearly established in England, we can now become interested in those Englishmen who soon were to leave the Old World for the New. We can become particularly interested in a certain English Separatist minister, a man named Roger Williams, who sailed for New England in search of a freedom he could not have at home.

# *The Baptists and the Making of the American Colonies*

On a February morning in 1631 the ship *Lyon*, two months out of London, dropped anchor in the harbor of Boston. On board were twenty passengers, among them a young minister, Roger Williams, and his wife, Mary. The morning was a cold one, and as the passengers waited for the ship to be readied for landing they could look out at this town of Boston they had come to, seeing no more than a settlement of log cabins scattered over three hills. The center of the town was a cow pasture and a frog pond, and people made their way over paths that had been beaten out by the hooves of cows and horses and by their own feet that trampled in the mud when it rained. Some of the passengers looked and saw only the town, but Roger Williams saw the promise of the freedom he sought.

This Roger Williams was probably the son of a shopkeeper or a merchant tailor in London. Some say he was born in the year that Queen Elizabeth died, 1603; some say it was a few years later. Whatever date he was born, he was still a boy when one day he caught the notice of Sir Edward Coke, the great jurist, possibly because Williams could use shorthand, a new invention that had been learned by only a few. The great lawyer, one of the greatest in England's history, helped young Williams through his early schooling, and continued his interest while the young man was at Cambridge University.

Perhaps it would be interesting to stop here and speculate a bit on how Roger Williams may have been touched by a man we have met before: Thomas Helwys. Williams was, of course, a child in 1611 when Helwys founded the first Baptist church in England; and he was not aware of this happening or that Helwys a year later had addressed the king. But there were men in England who did know of Helwys and of his beliefs, and they continued to attack the principle of government by the divine right of kings. One of these men was Sir Edward Coke, who, at the time of his association with young Williams, was defying James and drawing his ire, but was too powerful to be imprisoned as Helwys and many others had been.

Could it be that the great lawyer in talking with the boy told him of Helwys and of his courage, told of the myth of the divine right of kings, spoke of the worth and dignity of every man, and explained the meaning of independence? If Coke did talk in this way—and it is entirely likely that he did—then the seed was finding especially good soil in the mind and the heart of this boy, which is the way that enduring ideas and eternal truths, once they are recognized, are often passed on.

Roger Williams was a brilliant student at Cambridge, particularly in languages, mastering the use of Latin, Hebrew, French, and Dutch; and he took his degree in 1627. He was ordained a minister in the Church of England, but, so far as we know, he never functioned in the church and he found himself extremely restless in its confines. Williams first adopted Puritan principles; then, deciding that he opposed the union of church and state, went further and became a Separatist.

Unable to find the freedom of worship he wanted in England, young Williams—he could not have been more than twenty-eight—sailed in highest hope and idealism for the New World.

At this time there were two important colonies in America: one at Jamestown, Virginia, and another in Massachusetts. The people of the Virginia colony, founded in 1607, had come from the Cavaliers of England, royalists in their thinking; and in effect they brought their church with them, the Church of England. Continued in Virginia as the state church of the colony, it was the counterpart of the mother body in England.

The colony in Massachusetts was entirely different in its church background. The first people to settle in New England were *Separatists*—known to us as the Pilgrims—who landed at Plymouth in 1620. They were joined later in that decade by a number of other colonists, most of them *Puritans*, whose distinction, as you will recall, was that they would "purify" the Church of England of all its formal rites, particularly any suggestive of the Church of Rome. The two groups debated and prayed until they settled their differences, then they joined in forming a *Congregational* church in Massachusetts.

Even now, after all the years of research and study, no student or writer has been able to say why these men who had fled the state church in England founded exactly that same kind of church in New England. The Congregational church in Massachusetts was an established church, supported by enforced general taxation and governed by a combined state and church authority.

While the name suggests control by the congregation, any democratic practice in the church was cautiously watched by the authorities. It is one of the strangest of all contradictions that these men, who had set out seeking freedom of worship and conscience, should have gained this freedom, holding it completely in their own hands, and then have refused to accept it for themselves and at the same time denied it to all others.

It was to this colony that Roger Williams had come for the religious liberty that he could not find at home.

Any newcomer to the colony was made welcome, and the people gathered around Roger Williams to get the news from England. They found him to be a good talker, a minister, and they discovered that he was a man of learning. He went about the town observing its ways, and he attended services at the church. At the beginning of his stay he had nothing to say in the church.

At this time each church that could afford it had two ministers: one the minister of teaching and the other the minister of preaching. There was a need in the Boston church for a minister of teaching, and some of the elders got together and discussed the newcomer. He had had good schooling, was well mannered, and he seemed devout. Judging him too quickly because of their own need, and failing to discover the strength of his independence and the fire of his belief, they came to him and offered him the position.

They were astonished when he refused. They pointed out quickly that this was the First Church of Boston, the first church of America, and that the first families of America belonged to this church. Roger Williams told them that first principles came before a first church or first families, and that a man's conscience was more than any position, no matter what its pay or prestige. The infuriated elders left him, and soon some of the people came to ask why he had refused to serve.

He said that for all their talk of being Separatists they themselves had founded an unseparated church, which was completely in union with the civil government of the colony. Merely the fact that they, and not the Anglican bishops, controlled the church did not alter the fact that this established Congregational church was totally unscriptural in government, methods, and ordinances.

Williams told them that the charter which the Massachusetts Bay Colony had received from the King of England was invalid. These lands could not be given by the crown because they were not the crown's to give; they were the property of the Indians. He declared that the colony should return the charter to England as an accursed thing and should then meet with the Indians and make proper settlement, paying for the land that they had taken.

He went on to proclaim freedom of conscience and freedom of worship for every man, hammering at the foundation of authority both of church and state, and declaring that the magistrates had no right to try a man for breaking the Sabbath or for any other religious charge, that the magistrates were servants of the state only and had power over civil conduct only.

Williams was undermining the whole structure of joint church and state, and the people looked at him in horror. He was questioning their right to the land, touching their property and pocketbook, an even more dangerous thrust, and they turned from him as if he were the plague.

Shunned in Boston and hampered by the authorities, he received an offer to teach at a more liberal church in Salem. He accepted but had hardly begun his work there, when the elders began to talk among themselves. They had made an error, they felt, because this young man was speaking of religious liberty, of a free people in a free church. Soon, too, there came a letter, written jointly by the six leading men of Boston, addressed to the governor of Salem and warning him against the teachings of this dangerous Roger Williams. The people of Salem turned him out.

He went to Plymouth, the Pilgrim center—for had not these Pilgrims broken from the Church of England in order to have a free church? Surely his views would be welcome there.

For two years Williams remained at Plymouth, spending much of his time with the Indians, learning their ways and mastering their tongue, until he could converse with them freely and later could write *The Key into the Indian Language in America.* Something of Roger Williams' character is suggested by something he wrote: "My soul's desire is to do the natives good. God was good to give me a painful, patient spirit, to lodge with them in their filthy, smokey holes and to gain their tongue." It is said that he developed such a degree of friendship with the Indians, and so great was his influence among them, that if he had desired to make them merely nominal Christians, without their understanding the meaning of Christianity, they would have come to him as whole tribes to testify to their conversion.

Roger Williams spent most of his time with the Indians, but the watchful church leaders at Plymouth, having always suspected him, now finally proclaimed the danger of his views, and they turned against him. He went back to Salem, but the civil court there quickly ordered that he be dismissed from the church and that he keep silent.

So in 1634, after three years in the colony, he was really a man without a position of any kind. The governor, announcing that he would be lenient, then gave Roger Williams a chance to recant, to change his views and admit the errors in his teaching. Williams refused and repeated his belief in religious liberty, in the freedom of conscience for every man, and the right of a free people to worship in a free church. The governor banished him: "Mr. Williams shall depart from the jurisdiction of this colony within six weeks ensuing and not return any more without license from this court."

It was the dead of winter; Mary Williams was expecting a baby; and Roger Williams was himself in frail health at this time. So the court was merciful and said that he could stay until after the baby came, but he was not to appear in public and not to speak with anyone on matters pertaining to the state or the church or on any other matter that pertained to the general welfare.

This was the land to which he had come for religious freedom and these were the people who had left England because they had been persecuted. Yet here, where they were completely free to make whatever government or church they wished, they had welded the old laws of church and state into a new tyranny, exchanging one bondage for another, imprisoning those who did not conform, whipping those who dared to speak their disagreement, hanging the heretics, drowning the dissident ("drawing them into the water"), and burning the witches.

In their midst Roger Williams would not keep quiet. His baby was born and they named her Freeborn; and he went on preaching against intolerance and bigotry and injustice, saying that these evils were no less evil merely because this was a new country. Not all the people were against him, however, and some came to his home, asking for counsel which he gave. Spies came too, and the court was informed that the reports were true: He was speaking of the church and of the state. A secret order was then issued that he be arrested and sent back to England in chains, but he heard of the order and, as the officers were coming to take him, he slipped out of the back of his house and into the forest.

He spent that winter with the Indians, and in the spring four men who believed as he believed came to join him. With these men came Mary and his two children. They then crossed over into the country of the Narragansetts, and there one day, in 1636, they found a cool spring of fresh water. Williams called the place Providence and thanked God that He had brought them there.

He bought land from the Indians and said that he would found a colony dedicated to the principle of complete liberty of conscience. Twelve men and their families joined him; and they formed the first settlement in the area that later was called Rhode Island.

When Roger Williams adopted the principle of absolute soul liberty, he did not stop there; he continued to search the Word of God. He, like the others about him, had been christened as an infant. But as he and his friends studied the scriptures, they came to the belief that infant baptism was unwarranted and not the way of the New Testament church. Williams, therefore, declared that none of these people had been truly baptized.

Nowhere in the New World was there a church practicing believer's baptism. How, then, could they overcome this difficulty? How could they be baptized? Williams was the only minister in the group, and they decided to take the only course open to them. Ezekiel Holliman, who had been in the

Salem church, declared his new understanding and belief and he baptized Williams. Williams thereupon baptized Holliman and ten others in the month of March, 1639.

On that day, and at that place beside the spring called Providence, the first Baptist church in America was formed.

Every so often a ship came into Boston harbor with passengers who had sailed from England for reasons as varied as to escape prison or to have the right freely to acknowledge that Jesus is Lord. On one such ship there came Dr. John Clarke, a young physician of London, who felt that Christ was supreme and that English law interfered with his acknowledgment of that supremacy. He believed, as so many others had believed, as Roger Williams had believed, that in the New World he would have freedom of worship.

A man who viewed the New World as a haven of religious liberty could scarcely have come to a worse place than Boston in November of 1637. At this time Mrs. Anne Hutchinson, a daughter of an English rector who had turned nonconformist, was in grave conflict with the established church in Boston concerning doctrine. From the high pulpit of the First Church of the Puritans she was finally denounced as a woman of dangerous views and a servant of Satan. The civil magistrates then banished her and her brother from the colony.

John Clarke's shock at finding such as this going on in the New World was so great, and his sympathy for the woman and her brother so strong, that he and a small number of others followed them into banishment. He did not agree with the beliefs of Anne Hutchinson, but he felt so deeply about her right to hold to her beliefs that he was willing to join in her peril. Clarke soon became the natural leader of the group. While the founding of the first Baptist church in the New World was truly the work of Roger Williams, it is probable that John Clarke had a more enduring influence on the total Baptist fellowship in America.

The little group wandered, going first into New Hampshire and then, having endured a winter there, setting out again and traveling south until "to a town named Providence we came, which was begun by one Roger Williams, by whom we were courteously and lovingly received." Through Williams' mediation with the Indians, Clarke and his group were able to buy land and start a settlement. The group immediately drew up a contract among themselves dedicating their lives and their estates to Jesus Christ, and they made freedom an essential part of the new order. Popular sovereignty was instituted, and it was pledged that there would be no ruler in the community except the will of its people. They founded a place they called Newport.

John Clarke was made the preacher of the new church. Within the congregation were men and women who had been of different creeds but who now were firmly united in their common loyalty to Jesus Christ as Lord and Savior and in their devotion to the principle and practice of religious freedom.

We do not know when Dr. Clarke became a Baptist. It is thought, however, that in his discussions with Williams and others in Providence he had gradually adopted Baptist views concerning immersion of believers. He may not actually have been baptized until after he came to Newport; but wherever this took place, he and all members of his congregation were immersed, and they formed the second Baptist church in America.

The Baptist cause was progressing so rapidly in New England and the doctrine of believer's baptism, along with its accompanying denial of infant baptism, was becoming so common that the Massachusetts Colony felt it necessary to pass a law especially against the Baptists. So a law was put upon the statute books in 1644 that "since the first arising of the Anabaptists" they had been "troublers of churches" and had held the baptizing of infants to be unlawful along with other "errors and heresies." Furthermore, since they have appeared "among ourselves" in New England, it is, therefore, "ordered and agreed that if any person or persons within this jurisdiction shall openly condemn or oppose the baptism of infants, or shall go about secretly to seduce others from approbation or use thereof . . . every such person or persons shall be sentenced to banishment."

With the mention of the word Anabaptist, we must interrupt this narrative. The name was first used early in the fourth century against members of a group who insisted on "re-baptizing" those who came to them from the Church of Rome. Early in the next century the Theodosian Code provided the death penalty for Anabaptists. For centuries after this the name was used occasionally, and then it came fully into prominence once more in reference to a group of godly people in sixteenth-century Switzerland. It was intended as an accusation against them and an indictment of their practices.

These people in Switzerland were united by a plain and simple covenant, written by them after they had searched the Bible for themselves, without dictate of any church. Finally, with their Bibles open before them, they asserted that "the Scriptures teach nothing of infant baptism, and they who would be baptized according to God's word must first be believers."

They turned completely from the baptizing of an unknowing and helpless babe, looking on such a practice as without any possible meaning. Baptism, they said, could be truly received only by one who asks for it in the maturity of his own understanding and in the decision of his own belief. This was "believer's baptism."

These people called themselves by no other name than Christians or brethren; but those who opposed them and derided them, wanting to destroy them, gave them the name Anabaptists. It was not by chance that the name was given, for there is a carefully studied meaning in the word.

The prefix "ana" is Greek and means again or anew. So the opponents of this group were saying that its members, when baptized as grown men and women, were being baptized again or anew.

But the people themselves said that they were not being baptized anew, and for the very good reason that they had never been baptized before. The ritual at the time that they were infants, and could make no decisions for themselves, was merely something that the church had imposed on them. They argued that except for its form, it had nothing to do with baptism.

The deep significance of this position can be recognized when one takes into account that its acceptance would automatically make all those who believed in infant baptism actually unbaptized. Understanding this, one can understand the horror and the anger of those who clung to the practice, and their hatred of those who denied its meaning.

One can also understand the bitterness in the use of the term Anabaptist, how it became a reviling name and was used as a label against any and all nonconformists, no matter what their particular disagreement with the established church, and no matter how great the differences in their beliefs from those early Anabaptists, centuries ago, and those plain and godly people of Switzerland to whom the name was later given.

When the writers of the 1644 law in the Massachusetts Colony used the term Anabaptists they were doing it partly to decry the Baptists, partly to kindle and continue prejudice, and partly to bolster themselves and their position by the old and feeble device of belittling others.

The law against the Anabaptists was applied with vigor. The most celebrated case was that against Dr. John Clarke, Obadiah Holmes, and John Crandall. These three men, representing the Newport church, had traveled to Lynn, Massachusetts, at the invitation of some men who had adopted Baptist views and wanted to be baptized, and also to partake of the Lord's Supper in accordance with the Baptist way. As the small company was worshiping on Sunday in a private home, two constables came with a warrant for the arrests of "certain erroneous persons, being strangers."

They were taken to the state church where upon refusing to bare their heads the pastor commanded the constable to "pluck their hats off." John Clarke attempted to explain the reasons for their lack of respect for the established church, but he was refused a hearing. The three men were then accused of unlawful worship, disturbing public worship, and denouncing the established church as not being according to the "order of our Lord."

Some days later they were tried and sentenced. Clarke was sentenced to a fine of 20 pounds or, if he could not pay it, to be "well whipt." Holmes, because he had been repeatedly arrested for such acts was fined "30 pounds or to be well whipt." The sentence for Crandall was 5 pounds or to be "well whipt." Clarke's and Crandall's fines were paid, but Holmes refused to have his fine paid and suffered the penalty of whipping. Two men who expressed sympathy for him were arrested and fined.

In writing of the experience later, Clarke reported that during the examination the governor had upbraided them with the name of Anabaptists. Clarke denied this, saying that he had baptized many but had never *re*-baptized any. The governor then said: "You deny our former baptism, and make all our worship a nullity." Clarke's comment on this was: "I told him he said it."

This matter of making "all our worship a nullity" because of denying any meaning to infant baptism was the worst and most horrible of all the offenses, according to members of the established church, in the preaching of these Baptists. Indeed, at the trial of Clarke and the other Newport men, and just before sentence was imposed, John Cotton, the minister of Boston, "affirmed that denying infants' baptism would overthrow all; and this was a capital offense and therefore they were soul murderers." After Clarke and his associates had paid their fines, or taken the whipping, they returned to Newport and continued their worship.

It was some years later, in 1651, that Rhode Island needed a new charter; Roger Williams and Dr. Clarke sailed for England to get it. Williams remained in England for three years, then returned to America, leaving Clarke to manage the affair. It was not, however, until 1663 that Clarke finally secured the charter, and it then came from Charles II, a king of despotic tendencies who had been bitterly persecuting dissenters. Just how Clarke managed to get what he believed in and what he wanted is not known, but the charter he brought back to Rhode Island is one of the most remarkable, in regard to its provisions for civil and religious liberty, ever given by any sovereign.

Some two centuries later George Bancroft, the great American historian, was to say: "*To this charter belongs the first position as a state paper among the records of civilized man."*

The charter of Rhode Island, secured by John Clarke and probably written by him, declares: "That no person within the said colony, at any time hereafter, shall be anywise molested, punished, disquieted, or called in question for any difference in opinion in matters of religion which do not actually disturb the civil peace of said colony; but that all and every person and persons may from time to time, and at all times hereafter, freely and fully have and enjoy his and their own judgments and consciences in matters of religious commitments . . ."

When Clarke returned with the charter, properly sealed with the great seal of the King of England, he was received with honor. The charter became the touchstone of American democracy and was the basis for the subsequent First Amendment of the Constitution of the United States. To John Clarke belongs a great part of the honor of being the real founder of the Baptist movement in the New World; and he, along with Roger Williams, deserves to be remembered as the pioneer of the principle of religious liberty in the United States.

Up until this time, 1664, no Baptist church had been organized in the colonies outside of the Providence and Newport boundaries. Meetings were being held in Massachusetts, but persecution by the authorities made it impossible for the scattered groups of Baptists openly to manifest themselves as a church. Then John Myles, a Welsh Baptist minister, led a group of Welshmen from their native land to Rehoboth, Massachusetts. They were left alone for a while; then two of them were hauled before the court "for setting up a public meeting without the knowledge and approbation of the court." They were fined and ordered to desist from meeting in Rehoboth.

The first Baptist church in Boston was organized in 1665 in the home of Thomas Gould. Nine persons, including two women, solemnly covenanted together "in the name of the Lord Jesus Christ, to talk in fellowship and communion together, in the practice of all the holy appointments of Christ, which He had or should further make known to them." Fierce persecution confronted the tiny group and the court ordered them to desist from meeting. Nearly all of them were at one time or another imprisoned and fined, and Gould was imprisoned so frequently and for such long periods that his health was broken. Despite all this the group built a small meeting house on Salem Street and worshiped there, even though at one time the doors were nailed shut by order of the general court.

By 1671 the church membership had increased to twenty-two. Doubtless this increase came about because of the decline in the persecution of Quakers and Baptists around that time. The hanging of four Quakers had so aroused public indignation in England that the authorities there ordered Massachusetts to send any prisoners accused of religious offenses to England for trial. Upon receipt of this word, the Boston authorities promptly freed all religious prisoners and sent word back to England that they did not have any persons under arrest for religious reasons.

Twenty years later, in 1691, there was an easement for the Baptists. In the new charter given by William and Mary, drawing the Massachusetts Bay and Plymouth settlements into one colony, the Baptists were granted toleration. The charter is something of a tribute to the wisdom and to the religious sufferance of William and Mary, because the Baptists were still chopping at the knot that bound church and state, thereby chopping away at the joint authority of the two. They were also making "all our worship a nullity" and even acting as "soul murderers," because they were continuing to preach that infant baptism was not baptism.

It should be recognized, however, that while the charter did grant toleration to the Baptists and offered something of an assurance to them, they still had to pay the church tax and thus support an institution in which they did not believe.

In the latter half of the seventeenth century the Baptists slowly made their way into other places in the colonies. The first Baptist church in the South was established in Charlestown, South Carolina, about 1690. Before the century was out, Baptists were in New Jersey, New York, Pennsylvania, and the area that is now Delaware. Baptist teachings continued to spread throughout the colonies until, by the time of the War for American Independence, it is estimated that there were thirty-five thousand Baptists in America.

Baptists generally favored independence from Britain, and this put them in a favorable light with the other colonists and left them in a favorable position when the war was won. In fact, the independence movement offered an exceptional opportunity to the Baptists in their determination to gain religious liberty, for they could readily point to the impossible contradiction in the gaining of civil liberty bereft of religious liberty.

New York in 1777 promulgated a new constitution, which permitted "the free exercise of religious profession and worship without discrimination or preference." Eight years later Virginia established full religious freedom in a constitutional provision drawn up by Thomas Jefferson and strongly advocated by James Madison. Most of the other colonies, as they formed themselves into states, adopted provisions in their constitutions that guaranteed freedom of worship. Then, in 1789, came the culmination of the movement for religious liberty, when the Federal Constitution added its First Amendment, which provided that "Congress shall make no law respecting an establishment of religion, or prohibiting the free exercise thereof."

Even after this, some states, particularly in New England, kept the "churches of the standing order"; but Baptists and others who were not members of these churches received exemption from taxation for their support. It was not until 1833, however, that the last of the established churches was given up, when Massachusetts adopted a constitution which declared complete religious equality. Since that time every state in the Union has upheld the principle of separation of church and state, authorizing that those who believe in all forms of religions shall have the same rights and privileges, unless someone, by misusing the name of religion, acts against the peace and good order of society, as in the use of violence or physical corruption.

Thus, at last, a cardinal principle for which the Baptists had contended since their beginning in 1609—"The king is mortall man . . . and hath no power over ye immortall souls of his subjects . . ."—was at last firmly established as law in one nation on the earth. To America would come many who, in their own lands, had been deprived of their freedoms and denied the right to worship freely as they believed. America was now ready to give to the shackled of the earth the religious liberty which they craved and for which they prayed.

# *Frontier Days —and the Baptists Push On*

There is always adventure beyond the edge of a town and a touch of mystery in a thicket at the end of a road, and the men who settled New England, Pilgrims and Puritans in their faith but adventurers in their hearts, felt the lure of the land that stretched away before them. Some left their homes and moved out beyond the boundaries of the towns, clearing space for themselves, settling there and then watching others go by, seeing them pass and go on beyond, traveling west. The American frontier was forming and beginning to move toward the plains.

It continued to move while the wars with the Indians were fought, and while the great War for Independence was fought. By the time the new nation had been made, and the British were sailing home, the Americans in 1783 could claim the territory from New England across to the Mississippi River and south to Florida. As if this were not enough, leaders with vision and courage—already glimpsing the future perhaps, already seeing the full span of their nation—began adding to the land, dreaming vast dreams and making them come true, taking a continent in their stride.

Soon word began getting around in Europe about a nation where land was plentiful, and men began bundling their belongings and crowding into the holds of ships to get there. They came by the thousands and packed the cities of the East until they spilled over, and then the scattered traveling of individuals was ended and the full opening of the West began.

The settlers along the Eastern seaboard became accustomed to seeing the newcomers step ashore, hardly pause, and then travel on. They saw their friends and neighbors leave, heading West. They watched their own relatives pile their wagons high and set out, caught up in the excitement of the vast migration.

And then came a story out of India!

It may seem strange to turn abruptly from the American frontier and go to a setting so far away. But ours is the story of the Baptists, wherever the setting may be, and at this time, in the early days of the frontier, there came an account of happenings in far-away India that affected the Baptists and was to play a part on the American frontier.

The Hooghly River in the extreme eastern part of India is half a world away from the Mississippi River, but there was an event one day in 1800, in this broad and muddy stream of India, that had its influence in America.

A group of Baptist missionaries led by the great William Carey lived in the town of Serampore on the banks of the Hooghly; and they had tried at their mission to win the Indian people to Christ, but they had failed. Carey, who had started life as a mender of shoes and a bootmaker in England, had taken over the management of an indigo plantation to help support the work of the mission. He had translated the Bible into Bengali and taken long journeys into the jungles to tell the story of Christ to the people.

For seven years Carey and his associates—William Ward, Joshua Marshman, and John Thomas—had worked, and then came the day that they heard a cry for help: a man had injured himself. A carpenter—Krishna Pal by name, a Bengali by birth, and a Hindu by faith—had slipped and dislocated his shoulder. Dr. Thomas set it, binding it fast, and that afternoon the missionaries visited him. They asked if they might talk about their Lord, Jesus Christ, and if they might pray. The next day, and the next, and for many days the missionaries saw Krishna Pal, either in his own home or at the mission where he came for medical treatment.

Then came the time when he assembled his family and told them: "I have given my life to Jesus Christ and I am going to become a Christian." Quickly the word spread through the village and the people gathered. They beat the man and threatened him with death if he did not change his mind. But he would not change, and, on December 28, 1800, the first Indian convert of the modern missionary movement was baptized, the waters of the Hooghly covering him.

Later that same afternoon the group of missionaries and Krishna Pal sat down about the Lord's table, and for the first time the Bengali language was used in observing the Lord's Supper. This man in India was the first of millions who would follow him from almost every nation, going down into the waters of their native rivers for baptism.

Word of the happenings in India spread to New England, and soon in America there was a growing enthusiasm and dedication to foreign missions. Young men and women read of the baptisms in the Hooghly and they began to ask if the command to go forth and preach the Gospel to all nations did not apply to them. In the fervor of their missionary excitement they began to commit themselves. There was one in particular, Adoniram Judson, son of the pastor of the Plymouth Congregational church, who heard the call, and against the pleadings of his father he determined to go to foreign fields.

As the brig *Caravan* pushed its way out through the heads of Salem harbor on February 19, 1812, there were on board America's first foreign missionaries: Ann and Adoniram Judson and Samuel and Harriet Newell. Their destination was Calcutta, India.

Judson, ordained in the Congregational church, knew that he would meet the great Baptist missionary, William Carey, and meet the men who were associated with him, and he felt that he must prepare himself to answer their arguments against the baptism of infants. So he and his wife studied the Bible to find an answer to the question: "Ought children be baptized upon the strength of their parents' faith?" As they studied, they began to question the views of their own church, and by the time they reached Calcutta they had made their decision. They must, on profession of faith, seek baptism by immersion and become Baptists, even though this meant cutting themselves off from the church of their childhood and breaking the link with the newly organized Congregational Mission Board which had sent them out and had undertaken their support.

On their arrival in India they told their story to William Carey and the group at Serampore, and they were baptized in the Baptist chapel in Calcutta. On Carey's advice, Judson and his wife set out for Rangoon, in Burma, and there, on the highway to the Golden Pagoda, one of the most holy of all Buddhist shrines, Judson built a thatched-roofed hut and sat on the porch, inviting people to come in and talk. He talked of Jesus Christ, and despite threats, imprisonment, and torture he won men for Christ, and then he won more, and still more, until he established the great Baptist tradition in Burma.

At the time that the Judsons had been commissioned, there was another man sent out by the Congregational church, Luther Rice. He sailed on a later ship than the Judsons, but his experience on board was the same as theirs. He, too, closely studied the scriptures in regard to baptism, and on his arrival in Calcutta he affirmed the Baptist faith and was baptized by immersion.

Rice did not remain in India, but returned to the United States to win support for the Baptist missionary cause. He was so tireless and so fervent, constantly traveling, going from Maine to Georgia, that he was successful in 1814 in assembling thirty-three delegates from eleven states who gathered in Philadelphia to form a Baptist organization for foreign missions. It scheduled its meetings tri-annually, and thus became known as the Triennial Convention.

All the fervor for foreign missions, the work in India and Burma, the growing dedication to go forth and teach all nations, set some men to thinking about their own countrymen. What of their relatives and neighbors who had moved out to new land? What of them and their worship? There was work to be done at home, too, and missions were needed on the frontier.

Besides a growing concern for the spiritual life of the frontier, there began developing among the people of the Eastern seaboard one of those religious movements that sometimes grip a community, an area, a nation. Starting early in the 1800's, it became known as the Second Great Awakening.

America had had such an experience before. From 1725 to

1740 there had been a group of astonishing preachers in the colonies, and through continuous revivals they had kept the people in religious ferment. It was said of Jonathan Edwards, the pastor at Northampton, Massachusetts, that when he preached, the religious feeling became so intense in the church that many of the people had to hold on to the pews to keep from leaping into the air. The influence of his preaching was soon felt beyond the borders of his city and his state, and all New England was roused.

Then George Whitefield came from England to Georgia, taking up where John Wesley had left off in America. Whitefield preached his way up the coast and often moved inland to spread the Gospel. Immense audiences were attracted to him and in one stretch of 75 days he preached 175 times.

Gilbert Tennent and still other ardent evangelists rose to stand beside these men, and they lighted fires that burned in the South and throughout the East until this period of religious fervor became known, and is still spoken of, as the Great Awakening. These fires continued bright until they were smothered by the War for Independence and its hardships.

After the Revolution there was the usual disillusionment and cynicism that follow war, and then, slowly at first but growing in strength, the revivals began again. The Second Great Awakening, starting in the early part of the 1800's, lacked the ardor of the first because it lacked the eloquent and impassioned preachers, but its effect may have been more enduring because it was fostered through the work of average pastors in the South and the East.

A large number of converts were gained, and Christian life was extended and deepened. This was a time, too, when individuals and whole denominations were aroused to accepting new responsibilities. One responsibility that now became clear was the spiritual needs of the frontier, the call of home missions as well as missions abroad. The people were beginning to see that the great command to go forth and teach all nations was really a command to go and teach all men wherever they might be, whether in India or in settlements along the Ohio River, whether in Burma or Missouri.

The Baptist Gospel and the organization of the Baptist churches seemed to have been made for the frontier. The preaching was simple, having only a minimum of theology, and it emphasized a life-changing experience. The independence of each Baptist church and the right of every member to decide his faith for himself appealed to frontier democracy.

It was the frontier preachers, however, who made the greatest appeal, whether they were serving some local church as pastor or acting as missionaries and opening new ground in some far-off area of the frontier. They had been born and brought up as a part of the common people and their preaching did not separate them from the people. Most of the preachers labored during the week along with their congregations, and they expected little or no remuneration for their preaching. Their own belief and faith won the souls of these simple farmers and workmen to Christ, and it was this same faith that transformed them into preachers and gave them the desire to win others to their Gospel, whether they lived and preached in some settlement or traveled the frontier as missionaries.

It is a great and noble truth that before there was any real development of missionary organizations along the frontier, these warmhearted preachers rode the river barges and told the story of Christ to the other passengers and to the men who steered the barge. They got off at settlements and preached and handed out Bibles and literature. They borrowed wagons and rode as far as the trails were open. They then unhitched and rode horseback, and when a missionary could ride no farther he left his horse at some house. He then would rest a pole across his shoulders, a bag tied at each end filled with Bibles and booklets, and would set out again, walking now—a "colporteur," a neck porter, as they were called—to go still deeper into the frontier, taking the message of Christ wherever he could find a man to talk to.

In 1814 the America Baptists organized their foreign missionary society in Philadelphia to meet the needs of the Judsons in Burma; but one year later Luther Rice, the inspiration for the work in the foreign field, was urging the Foreign Mission Board to act quickly and send missionaries to the Missouri territory. But the Board, organized to support only foreign missions, had no authority for missions at home. In 1817, however, at the second Triennial Convention, the constitution was altered, allowing the Board "to appropriate a portion of their funds to domestic missionary purposes, in such part of this country where the seed of the word may be advantageously cast." A new understanding and conviction was then expressed, that "western as well as eastern regions are given to the Son of God as an inheritance, and that His Gospel will triumph amidst the settlers of the Mississippi and in Missouri, and extend to the red inhabitants of the wilderness."

The most famous of the missionaries of the frontier was John Mason Peck. Peck was a native of Connecticut, with little formal schooling; but he taught school, and in 1813, at the age of twenty-four, he was ordained a Baptist minister by the church at Catskill, New York. He soon gave evidence of a deep missionary interest, and a meeting with Luther Rice set his heart on fire for the frontier. After a year in seminary training he became the real pioneer Baptist apostle to the

West. From the time of his appointment until his death at the age of seventy-nine he traveled the wilderness trails. Whenever, at intervals, he settled for any time, it was in one of the tough new towns of the Western prairies.

Peck's journey began in 1817 from his home in Litchfield, Connecticut, when he loaded a one-horse wagon with beds, trunks, and food. Then he, his wife, and their baby bumped down the road toward Missouri. For 125 days they traveled, and at last they crossed the Mississippi River and found themselves in St. Louis.

St. Louis then stood literally at the edge of civilized America. Beyond were the almost unmarked prairies, the really wild West, the Rocky Mountains, and Spanish California. The town was an unruly settlement with no school or church. Almost every building seemed to be a saloon, a gambling house, or a house of prostitution. It was so crowded with its population of tough men and the flow of its drifters that Peck and his family could find only one room in which to live.

He set up his home in that room. He found a place at the back of a store and there he started a school. There, too, he began to preach. And so the American Baptists had now moved west of the Mississippi, and were working at the edge of the frontier.

Peck taught and he preached. He saw some men glare at him and he heard their ridicule, but he sang his hymns and he prayed. Sometimes the room was empty, but still he preached and he prayed. Sometimes there were one or two to listen, hanging back, glancing about to see if they were seen. Still he preached, and it was two months later that he walked down into the water with his first convert; and it was the water of the Mississippi that opened and closed over the bearded man.

Through the heat of summer and the snow and ice of winter Peck traveled the length and breadth of the territory on horseback, his saddle bags heavy with Bibles and tracts. The settlers called him the mounted man of God and they welcomed him to their cabins. He never left a cabin without a prayer and without giving some portion of the scripture or a piece of Christian literature.

Illness slowed him, for he was a frail man, but schools and churches grew up to mark the path where he had traveled. He founded a seminary and he started a weekly newspaper, the *Western Pioneer*, and for years he edited it to help train church members in his far-reaching parish. Other missionaries followed him, spreading his work and continuing his teaching of the Gospel. So significant was his contribution to American Christianity that on one of his trips East Harvard University gave him the degree of Doctor of Divinity.

There is a curious pleasure and an enduring satisfaction in this particular degree. It was more than a degree to a man; it was the rectification of an error and a recognition of eternal truths.

Two hundred years before, in 1640, Henry Dunster came from England to Boston to become the leading candidate for the presidency of a new college that had recently been established; this was Harvard College. He became the first president of Harvard College, and then, twelve years later, he was dismissed because he had accepted Baptist views and had publicly declared that infant baptism was unscriptural. When Dunster appealed to the Overseers of the College, who had voted to be rid of him, to be allowed to remain in the house that he himself had built as the president's house, at least until the end of the hard winter, they had refused him and they turned him out.

This was the same Harvard College and Harvard University that in 1852 recognized the achievements of a frail man who, emboldened by God, had found the almost unbelievable strength and faith to defy the frontier and conquer it. This man was a Baptist and held the same views as had Henry Dunster. A great university was setting forth a new page and in it acknowledging clearly the rights of all men to the freedom of their faith.

# 1845: The Division

In a stagecoach, traveling between Richmond and Petersburg, Luther Rice had an idea he believed so right that he set himself the task of carrying it out. He thought that the Baptists lacked a national organization and that they needed one. At the time he was recently back from India and was traveling along the Eastern seaboard to acquaint the Baptists with the work of the Judsons and to tell of the general opportunities for foreign missions. Rice's plan was for the Baptists to come together in a great national convention to decide their mission policies.

The idea caught on at once and in May, 1814, the convention was held in Philadelphia. Popularly called the Triennial Convention and organized solely for the advancement of foreign missions, it was the first time that the Baptists of America had come together on a national basis and had united in a single national body.

They had no sooner organized, however, than the lines

of division began to form and to point to the cleavage of 1845.

The first disagreement came when the Convention, at its second Triennial meeting in 1817, voted to increase its activities and to undertake home missions as well as foreign missions. The disagreement was not about missions themselves but about any expansion of the Convention's authority. Some leaders wanted the Convention to grow into a truly representative denominational body, assuming supervision of all benevolent activities. Others, opposing any possible suggestion of centralized authority, insisted on a separate and distinct organization for each activity. At the third meeting of the Convention, in 1820, this latter group managed to get control and to hold the business of the Convention to foreign missions only.

The division, while important in regard to Baptist organization and jurisdiction, would not be nearly so significant were it not for the fact that the break was along sectional lines. The Southern churches below the Potomac approved, as a whole, the central organization. Those of the North wanted an individual organization—"societies," they came to be called—for each activity.

So it was that powerful and disruptive sectional forces, already showing up economically and politically between the North and the South, already being felt throughout the nation, were now coming in a roundabout way, through the matter of jurisdiction, to be felt by the Baptists.

In the disagreement the Northern group prevailed and the policy of individual societies was adopted. In 1824 the American Baptist Publication Society was organized for the purpose of distributing tracts and the printed Gospel.

In 1832 a third general group was formed, the American

Baptist Home Mission Society, this one with the purpose of carrying on missionary work in North America.

The Baptists of the South made it very plain that their plan for a central organization had nothing to do with the starting of any central church or the founding of any central authority. The organization they advocated would be concerned with benevolent activities only. It was their belief that these activities could be better planned, financed, and carried out, preventing overlapping and even conflict, if they were under the direction of a central planning body. The body itself would be acting solely as an instrument and a servant of the individual churches and would have no authority whatsoever except that authority voted by the churches themselves.

The Northern position, however, was maintained. In addition, the headquarters of the different societies were kept entirely in the North. The headquarters of the General Mission Convention, having to do with foreign missions, was in Boston. The American Baptist Home Mission Society headquarters was in New York. The Executive Board of the American Baptist Publication Society established itself in Philadelphia. Travel being what it was in those days, Southern representation at the meetings of the boards was never great, even though there were more Baptists in the South than in the North.

In 1835 the division between the Northern and Southern groups was further widened. The specific issue in this case concerned home missions. The Southerners pointed out that the Home Mission Society, three years after it was organized, had sent no missionary at all into Kentucky, Alabama, Louisiana, or Florida; and had sent only one into Mississippi, three to Tennessee, and three to Arkansas—a total of seven for six states and a territory. The average was one missionary for every 400,000 persons. They then pointed out that Michigan alone had sixteen missionaries, and that in Michigan, Illinois, and Indiana there was one missionary for every 4,000 persons—a ratio of 100 to 1 in favor of the North.

In reply, the Society, which was recruiting its missionaries in New England and New York, said that they could find no missionaries who were willing to work in the heat of the deep South. The Southerners mentioned the heat of India and Burma, saying that men gloried in going there; and they asked if sectionalism was playing its unhappy part even in the work of missions.

The issues that finally separated Northern and Southern Baptists in 1845 were, in part, those issues already mentioned; but there were other causes, and much older causes, that went far deeper. As is almost always the case in religious matters, the secular background was playing its part. The immediate occasion for the break was the difference in regard to missions and who would be accepted as missionaries; but beyond this was the fact that these men in disagreement were Southerners and Northerners, as well as Baptists, and were involved in the intense sectionalism of the period, especially in the question of slavery.

Slavery was not an open divisive issue among Baptists prior to 1830. As a matter of fact, they displayed, as early as 1789, a general readiness to question the validity of slavery as a practice among Christians. In Virginia the Baptist General Committee in that year adopted a resolution calling upon the legislative assembly of the state to abolish slavery gradually. Four years later, however, the committee decided to dismiss the subject, yielding to the pressure of some associations that advised leaving the issue to the individual conscience.

A similar caution was evident among Maryland Baptists. In Kentucky, associations sought to side-step the issue, but were unable to prevent the formation of emancipation parties in churches led by abolitionist preachers. As a consequence, slavery divided Kentucky Baptists for the first thirty years of the nineteenth century. In South Carolina, where one-third of the Baptist laymen and two-fifths of the ministers were slaveholders, it was difficult to make a pronouncement of any kind on slavery. Throughout the South most Baptists were anxious to preserve unity and to avoid offending the slaveholding members of their churches; but the issue became increasingly difficult as abolitionists of the North grew ever more insistent on arousing public opinion and in demanding that the slaves be freed.

Under the sting of this Northern propaganda some Southern Baptists, particularly in South Carolina and Virginia, began to defend the institution of slavery; though most Baptist leaders in the South, during the 1820's and 1830's, tried to keep peace by following a policy of moderation. Open controversy, however, could not be avoided in a nation torn by sectional differences, with all the interplay of their economic, political, social, and religious overtones. The slavery question, successfully suppressed among Baptists until April, 1840, finally came completely into the open when the American Baptist Anti-Slavery Convention was organized in New York City and expressed its unreserved opposition to slaveholding.

This was a comparatively small group but its action was noted in the South, and the Alabama Baptist Convention informed the Board of Foreign Missions of the General Convention in November, 1840, that it would withhold all funds until the Alabama Baptists were assured that the Board had no connection with abolitionism. The Board's reply was an evasion, a statement that its members as individuals might act as they wished, but that as officials of the Convention they had no right to do or say anything with respect to slavery. Although this position satisfied neither abolitionists nor slaveholders, the Alabama Convention's fears were allayed for the time being.

When the General Convention met in Philadelphia in 1844 an attempt was again successfully made to side-step any consideration of the slavery issue. The South, however, by now was ready for a showdown, and, a few days after the Convention's adjournment, the Georgia Baptist Convention instructed its executive committee to recommend to the Board of the Home Mission Society the appointment of James E. Reeves of Georgia as a missionary to the Cherokee Indians. Reeves was a slaveholder and the request was obviously a test case. After several extended meetings of the Board the decision was seven to five against appointing Mr. Reeves.

This response, along with other disturbing events, led the Alabama Baptist Convention in November, 1844, to challenge the Foreign Mission Board's decision to retire Jesse Bushyhead, a highly respected Indian preacher, because he owned slaves. The challenge was in the form of a Resolution insisting that the Foreign Mission Board give slaveholders and non-slaveholders the same privileges. In December the Board replied that it could not appoint any candidate who had slaves and who insisted on retaining them as his property, for this would imply approval of slavery.

The die was rapidly being cast, for there was increasing evidence that the abolitionist sympathizers were gaining the upper hand. There had already been talk about separation between the Northern and Southern groups but now, after the reply to the Alabama Resolution, the Virginia Baptist Foreign Mission Society decided upon action and issued a call for a convention to meet in Augusta, Georgia, "on Thursday before the 2d Lord's day in May next." Some three hundred delegates answered the call and there in the Georgia city in May, 1845, the division was no longer debated. Instead, the organization of the Southern Baptist Convention was begun.

A fact that should be clearly understood, and emphasized, is that the division was in regard to benevolent activities. There was not any serious denominational distinction. The decision was simply that the Northern and Southern churches would carry on their work in separate groups, each organized along lines that it preferred. Each would maintain its own home and foreign missions. Each would determine and carry out its own policies in regard to all benevolent and general activities. None of this, however, was intended to affect the basic union in Baptist beliefs and faith.

At the first meeting in Augusta, at the very forming of the Southern Baptist Convention, this spiritual unity was emphasized in the Address to the public. It was said then that: "Northern and Southern Baptists are still brethren. They differ in no article of the faith. They are guided by the same principle of gospel order . . . We do not regard the rupture as extending to foundation principles, nor can we think that the great body of our northern brethren will so regard it."

The division, however, continues and since that time other Conventions have been formed, among them the National Baptist Convention of America and the National Baptist Convention, USA, Inc., with their eight million members, the largest bodies of church membership of Negroes in the world.

Some of the Conventions of today differ in ways that are more than organizational. These differences may have to do with social practice. They may be concerned with questions of theology or church membership. Whether the differences are lessening or not can be debated, but there is one magnificent and enduring fact which cannot be debated, and that is the great spiritual union in which all Baptists are joined. In this union is the basic purpose and prayer that every man shall come to a personal acknowledgment of Jesus Christ as Lord and Savior, that every man, through grace, shall find "a way home."

The Baptist past was an exciting one but now, as we turn to their work today, the threat of prison and fear of the hangman are gone. The story may seem less dramatic than when Roger Williams fled into the forest or Obadiah Holmes was "well whipt"; but there are religious liberties still to be won, churches to be founded, and souls to be saved. The work of the Baptists now is just as meaningful as then, and the accounts that follow make up a fascinating record of the dedicated and determined efforts of Baptists to carry out their responsibilities today and to continue their courageous tradition.

# THE BAPTIST STORY TODAY—THEIR WORKS AND THEIR WAYS

# *The Training of Their Ministers*

Sydnor L. Stealey
President
1951-1963
Southeastern Baptist Seminary

The graduates of the county high school sat, dignified and self-conscious, in their assigned places on the platform, the girls in spotless white dresses and the boys in dark coats and ties. Seated in the front row, and partly hidden by the flowers, were those who were to take part in the exercises: the valedictorian, the school principal, the county superintendent, and the two ministers who would give the invocation and the benediction. This year, by coincidence, both ministers were Baptists. Both were completely respected in their churches and in the community and no one distinguished between them or held one above the other, either in regard to character or to work. There was one difference, however, which is not paramount in the judging of a man but which, in our discussion of seminaries and the training of ministers, should be mentioned. One of these pastors was a Doctor of Philosophy, a graduate of Yale University. The other never finished grade school.

A Baptist minister a Doctor of Philosophy? Yes. A Baptist minister from a grade school? Yes. There is no set level of education for Baptist ministers and no fixed educational requirement whatever.

Thousands of Baptist ministers over the country, like the one on the platform, have graduate degrees—Doctor of Philosophy, Doctor of Theology—which they have earned at the great schools in this country and abroad. Other Baptist ministers, preaching every Sunday and serving their congregations well, never finished sixth-grade grammar school. Furthermore, in the independence of each Baptist church, if a congregation decided to ordain a man who had never gone to school at all, who had taught himself to read and write, they could call him straight from the plough. Uneducated mill hands and farmers, working at looms or ploughing throughout the week, are preaching at some of the smaller Baptist churches on Sunday and are serving them sincerely; but the trend to have educated Baptist ministers is up, sharply up. Many Baptist churches now are speaking out for higher standards in the training of ministers, asking that a man be at least a seminary graduate, and some churches are insisting that their pastors have a Doctor's degree. The trend, as I say, is decidedly up.

Moreover, the trend is having a marked effect on the course of study of young men preparing themselves for the Baptist ministry. There are many of these dedicated young men now in colleges and universities who will go on to the great graduate schools—Harvard, Yale, Princeton, Chicago. Others will attend seminaries for their graduate work.

There are some twenty Baptist theological seminaries in the United States, and a young man going into the ministry will select one of them. Let us suppose that he looks the country over—and let me put all modesty aside and say that he chooses the seminary with which I was associated for so long, the

Southeastern Baptist Theological Seminary at Wake Forest, North Carolina. This selection allows me to write with a greater knowledge than if he had gone to some other seminary with which I am not so familiar. Then, too, while Baptist seminaries may differ somewhat in organization and curriculum, perhaps in some procedures, they do not differ in the basic requirements of faith, ideals, and purpose. So, for the sake of convenience and clarity, we will let our young man come to Southeastern Seminary, which can serve, at least as an indication, for them all.

In seeking admittance to the seminary the candidate must first be recommended by some church as worthy. He must have health references and indicate a seriousness of intent. He will present his college degree and his academic record, which will be checked by us. Then, having met our requirements, he will begin his studies and aim most often at the basic theological degree, Bachelor of Divinity, requiring three years. He will study Archaeology, Old Testament, New Testament, Church History and Christian Classics, Christian Missions, Theology, Philosophy of Religion, Ethics, Preaching, Speech, Religious Education, Music, Sociology, and Pastoral Care.

While study for this degree is on the graduate level it is not primarily in the character of research. Work at a seminary is more like work at a medical school, where students combine classroom studies with practical experience in laboratories and hospitals. Most Baptist seminary students gain their experience while serving as ministers in small churches or as assistant ministers in larger churches.

At Southeastern we have some five hundred and fifty students. Perhaps four hundred and forty work in churches located near enough to the seminary for them to travel back and forth between their student-ministerial duties and their classes. Frequently some church in our area, too small to require or afford a full-time minister, will call one of our students as its pastor. Frequently, too, our Director of Field Work will hear of a church in need of help and will recommend a student.

Work as a student minister usually requires considerable time and it frequently adds to a man's years at the seminary, perhaps doubling them and requiring six years for the Bachelor of Divinity. Suppose that later, and in addition to the B.D., he wants a Master of Theology degree. It is possible for him to take the M.Th. in one additional year; but classroom work, the thesis, and his work as a student minister usually stretch the time into two or even three years. As for the doctorate, I don't remember offhand anybody who ever took the Doctor of Theology degree in its minimum of two years after the B.D.

Expenses at all seminaries are held to the absolute minimum, both fees and living expenses. Also, there are Student Aid Funds and Loan Funds to help young men when both ends don't quite meet. Rarely is any seminary student well-to-do, and most of them have a hard time financially; but with some income from their ministerial duties and with help, perhaps from their homes or home churches, and with what aid and loan assistance we can give, they manage to make it.

There are women at Baptist seminaries taking the same courses as men. However, they usually specialize in religious education or missions rather than pastoral responsibilities, for I know of no Southern Baptist church with a woman preacher, and would risk a guess that none is likely to call a woman soon.

Baptist seminaries are integrated and at none of them, so far as I know, is there any official distinction or personal separation between Negro students and white students.

A seminary faculty usually is chosen by the President, who makes recommendations to the Board of Trustees. The Board, through its Committee on Instruction, examines every nominee carefully. Particular care is shown at present because of theological disagreements within the denomination.

The old way of teaching the Bible verbatim, which was common in the past, is now being discussed and challenged, and some seminaries are willing to examine critically the background of any passage and to consider new interpretations. The disagreement in seminaries and throughout the theological world is about how much of this critical approach is permissible. The stand that a man takes in regard to this issue is a prime reason for the Board's showing such care about anyone recommended for the faculty. They want to be sure about his views, not that they wish them necessarily to conform entirely with the predominant beliefs at the seminary but they do want his teachings not to be at such variance from the rest of the faculty that serious friction might come about.

Seminary teachers are selected for scholarship, for theological and spiritual qualifications, for their standards of teaching and their ability to require the most serious dedication from their students. Many a young fellow who loafed a bit or played a bit as an undergraduate puts aside his youthful ways at the seminary and gets down to the hardest kind of study. Then, too, many of the seminary students are married and this, of course, can influence the seriousness of a man's work—usually for the better, though sometimes for worse!

Most of our students come to us already ordained. A young man, while still an undergraduate at some college or university, decides that he wants to be a Baptist minister and he makes his decision known to the congregation of his church. His request is considered and he is judged. If the congregation approves, even though he be only a junior or senior in college, they will ordain him. Some of our students do come to us without being ordained, but often they join a church near our campus and a number of them have been ordained by these churches.

We are sometimes asked about special training for students in regard to weddings, funerals, baptizing. Actually, any man the day he has been ordained may have to step up and marry a couple. He may have to conduct a funeral. In such circumstances he refers to his "Minister's Manual," a little booklet that has marriage ceremonies and funeral forms in it, and with this he just does the best he can.

At the seminary we have a course on church administration in which we try to give some help on marriages, funerals, baptisms, and the Lord's Supper. If we have a student who is an older man, perhaps long a minister and already experienced before he came to us, we try to refine what he is doing. Of course, we try to help the inexperienced, but often they just go out and observe in churches, finding out in a practical way how to marry a couple, conduct a funeral, or baptize.

There are no fraternities at Baptist seminaries. There are games of various kinds, but no serious inter-school athletics. Our social life is enjoyable yet there is not a great deal of it, because a man's studies and his work as a student minister take up his time.

The seminary life that I have been describing is lived by about ninety per cent of our students, but besides these students working for advanced degrees there are others. They are enrolled because of a Baptist tradition dating back more than a century that any man who meets his *church requirements* should be admitted to a seminary despite a lack of academic preparation.

The tradition began with a very remarkable man, James P. Boyce, who is chiefly responsible for the founding of the great seminary at Louisville. Boyce argued, as early as 1856, against a belief "that the work of the ministry must be entrusted only to those who have been classically educated." Ministerial qualifications, he said, did not necessarily include knowledge "of the sciences, nor of philosophy, nor of the languages, but of God and His plan of salvation. He who does not have this knowledge, though he be learned in all the learnings of the schools, is incapable of preaching the Word of God." Boyce declared that from earliest time "the mass of vineyard workers" have been from the ranks of fishermen and tax gatherers, cobblers and tinkers, weavers and plowmen "whom God has qualified as His ambassadors by the presence of [His] spirit."

Behind Boyce's teaching "that the work of the ministry must *not* be entrusted only to those who have been classically educated" was an old, old reason, infinitely deep rooted, forever sharp and grinding in the minds and hearts of the Baptists. They had once been cobblers and tinkers, weavers and plowmen, and they had stood up against the combined strength of state and established church, and with their blood and their bodies they had paid for their religious convictions.

Baptists knew—they had heard it from their fathers, the narrative and the record continuously passed on—how men, six hundred years ago, five hundred, four hundred years ago, had died for translating the Bible from the learned tongues of statesmen and the state church into the language of the people. Pursued, persecuted, and burned, they had lighted a flame with their bodies, and others like them had taken up the risk of prison and death that the Book might be read by every plowboy. And the plowboy, in his time, when caught reading the Holy Book was also punished and imprisoned. This persecution was carried out by men of state and church, bred at the universities and steeped in classical learning. The Baptists, and all Nonconformists, were determined that neither in England, nor in the American Colonies, nor in the present American states would they ever permit the power of state or government to control them in their worship. Nor would they permit any learning, either lay or church, to be the deciding factor for their ministers or for recognition among themselves.

In Boyce's plan of training Baptist ministers he made his ideas quite clear. He would advocate the teaching of classical studies and urge proficiency for ministers in these studies, but he would not require them. He did not intend to weaken or water down the quality of ministers or to minimize the benefits of training; his purpose was to open ministerial opportunities to all men regardless of educational background, so that there would be more preachers, pastors, and missionaries to meet the steadily increasing demand for them. He did not believe it is "the business of the church to establish a perfect," but rather to establish an adequate ministry. And of these adequate ministers he wanted "an abundant supply."

This tradition continues despite the advancing educational requirements for Baptist ministers, and today we still fill ten percent—about fifty men—of our enrollment with students who have not completed college. Some have completed only high school. They take special courses, usually excluding Latin, Greek, Hebrew, and all other languages. They study for two years and then, having completed the special course planned for them, they receive a certificate, not a degree.

There are age limitations for these students. If a candidate is under thirty he must go to some college for an A.B. degree, then return to us for his B.D. If he is over fifty we make sure that he is capable of seminary work and that he is serious, intending to go out later and preach. He must not have the mistaken idea that at his time of life, and no matter how hard he has labored in the vineyard of the Lord, he can come to this pleasant academic atmosphere with its grassy lawns and shady trees and just rest awhile.

Some three per cent of our seminary students, whether studying for degrees or certificates, drop out each year. Some of them leave for financial reasons at home, or in their personal lives, or because of sickness. Others leave because of theological difficulties. They may come to us with a somewhat limited background, having had the teaching of only one preacher or possibly two in some very limited community. Then at the seminary they encounter theological thought from Germany, from England, South Africa, India, and sometimes they say: "We don't want any of this." And so they leave.

These two groups are not alone. There are others who go. They are the young men of confused mind and emotional disturbance. They, who once were so certain, have looked at the ministry anew and they wonder. In a lack of spiritual surety there comes a wavering of the call to preach.

The whole trend of modern life is secularistic and this is bound to have its influence on the lives of young men, even those who once were so sure of themselves. The national government is forever emphasizing the need for scientific training. Great businesses each year send out their representatives to visit the colleges and solicit their graduates. Any number of young men who have gone through college preparing for the ministry have been derailed because they showed special abilities in mathematics or science or languages and somebody has said to them: "Why, son, you can make three times as much in our business as you can make preaching. With what you earn in business, you can support two preachers. Come on in with us." This leads to confusion of thinking, and not infrequently to a change of purpose.

Nor is the secularistic influence the only one that is disturbing the young men of today. There is another force that is playing its part in the lives of the young men who waver. To be a Baptist, say no more than twenty years ago, you subscribed to just a few things and they were all settled and sure. But now, just about every one of them is being challenged. As an old man said not long ago: "Everything that was nailed down is done come up."

First of all, you believed in God. God was very indefinite but at the same time was very concrete. He was the God that the preacher told you about. Whatever the preacher said about Him, you believed. God was love. God forgives you this instant. You want to be saved, don't you? Come on down and join the church. That was pretty shallow maybe, but you didn't question it.

The concepts of Christ and the Bible were also firm and hard, and they too were accepted without question. The theory of the inspiration of the scriptures was not questioned. If you did question it you were pretty soon cast out. In order to be a Baptist you believed in certain teachings and there was no doubt in you. But today some of our bright young men come in and they want to talk. They cannot subscribe to the old set creed or confession or statement of faith. And yet, they believe in God. They believe that Jesus, as they understand Jesus, is revealing the truth about life. We welcome the chance to talk to these serious students and help them resolve their questions. Many of them have gone on to become outstanding ministers.

Then, too, the young ministerial and seminary students are faced with this matter of integration and it is playing an increasing part in their thinking. I know of no student at this seminary who does not support the justice and morality of integration, and many of them say that they will not preach in a church that does not let them preach their convictions. Because of this matter of segregation some of the finest young men in the seminary are veering away from the pulpit, not wanting the strain and conflict that would meet them in some churches. They are becoming chaplains—military chaplains, hospital chaplains, institutional and industrial chaplains. Some few are changing denominations.

But whatever the trial for these men may be, or however difficult the burden for them or others, there is always an enduring incentive to the Baptist ministry. It is in the urgency of a man's conviction that God in Christ has shown us how to live. This is what we must go out and tell. This is the deepest incentive I know, and it can overcome all worries and all doubts.

It is my faith that what we know of God we know primarily through Jesus. This is a pretty big thing sometimes. God is Spirit. God is Love. God is Father. These are rather vague statements if we really think about them. God is a blanketing term and the theologians recognize this more and more. Some of them call Him the Ultimate, the Essence of Being, and various other phrases that indicate His vastness, His incomprehensibility to the human mind. But they say that what we know about living in a right relationship with the Ultimate Being, with God, we know through Jesus. I feel this very deeply.

Love must cast out hate. We must take time to be holy. We must study to show ourselves approved. We must find God's way, and we find it primarily through Jesus. This is the basic belief of a student preparing himself at the seminary. This is the basic belief of an intensely serious Baptist minister. This is a belief that any man can live by, and live with forever.

# *Their Home Missions*

Courts Redford
Executive Secretary-Treasurer
Home Mission Board
Southern Baptist Convention

There is a verse in Matthew—28:19—that is the marching order for Foreign Missions. "Go ye therefore, and teach all nations, baptizing them in the name of the Father, and of the Son, and of the Holy Ghost." And a moment later Jesus said: "And, lo, I am with you alway, even unto the end of the world." This order is clear and thousands of missionaries have heard it and carried it out.

There is another verse, this one in Mark—1:38—that is not so well known but it also has its message: "Let us go into the next towns, that I may preach there also," Jesus said.

One does not have to go to the end of the world. There are missions here at home, in "the next towns." The setting may not be glamorous or the trip far, but the work of Home Missions is at any man's hand. Moreover, he need not travel to the end of the world to find people of other backgrounds, if these are the ones he seeks. They have come to him; in our country today there are twenty-five million foreign-speaking people.

There are two million migrant laborers in the United States who go seasonally from area to area, from crop to crop—but do they go from church to church? Twenty-five thousand communities in this country have no Baptist church. Young people by the thousands want teaching and guidance. Hospitals, military camps, institutions, and industries are asking for chaplains. Foreign missions? There is infinite work, and noble work, in foreign countries. There is also work here at home, so much work, so great a need.

At one time, say a century and a half ago, the need for home missions and home missionaries stood out plainer than now. Across the continent, strange and unknown to us, lived a people unknown to us, the Indians; and the mission call was almost like the call to a foreign land. In Eastern cities the European immigrants lived in crowded surroundings, perplexed and lonely, in poverty and spiritual need. In the South the slave worked in the fields and worshiped as he could. Home missions then was an open and obvious challenge.

It is not so obvious now, and this is partly because the story of the home missionary is not often told. Did you ever read about the missionaries who work among the 250,000 deaf people in the United States? Ever read about Baptist missionaries who *today* live and work among the American Indians? Ever even hear about our missionaries who travel ahead of the agricultural migrants, getting Sunday Schools and churches ready for them when they arrive to harvest the tomatoes, the wheat, the apples? A good many people don't know very much about home missions; but there are others who do, men and women who talk with us on flying fingers, a Mexican child in a California Sunday School hearing a Spanish-speaking teacher, an old and mentally unstable woman in a hospital listening to a chaplain; they know about us.

What is the work of home missions? What do we do? How

do we do it? Actually, home missions is an organized effort of all our churches to accomplish what a single church, or possibly a group of churches, cannot accomplish. The average church cannot provide a language ministry or a ministry for the deaf or a center designed to serve the underprivileged of a community. Such undertakings then become the responsibility of all the churches combined, and this joint organization is the Home Mission Board.

With Baptists, the individual church is paramount, and each Baptist church, pine and whitewashed or made of marble, is independent. Each church does what it wants, except when it wants something beyond its experience or organization or income. Then, quite likely, the Home Mission Board may be called on to help. Most of our work is done in co-operation with a church, an Association, or a State Convention. In fact, many of our missionaries are considered both State and Home missionaries, supported jointly by the two organizations.

A Baptist missionary, however supported or wherever he may be, has one purpose. In Burma, in the Congo, in the Andes a missionary is always asking how can he win the unsaved. How can he baptize them and enlist them in Christian witnessing? A Baptist missionary riding the plains of Texas or a packed subway in New York is asking how can he advance the Kingdom of God? We Baptists are an evangelical denomination, and evangelical means "to bear a message of glad tidings." These are the tidings that a Baptist missionary constantly bears, whether in foreign lands or at home, forever telling of full surrender to Christian service.

Besides dealing directly with people, there are other ways to fulfill a mission. The founding of new churches is one of them, and this is a very important part of the over-all evangelical plan. The Home Mission Board is very much concerned with starting new churches because as these churches move out, each going beyond another, they advance the Baptist mission. This, too, is a way of going into the next towns to preach the Gospel.

The founding of a new church is a most serious undertaking, and the Home Mission Board makes numerous surveys of population centers and trends as a part of the necessary study and preparation. Once a survey shows where a church is needed, this information is passed on to the local churches, and one of them will become the sponsoring church. The actual start probably will be with a Sunday School, the mother church holding meetings in a borrowed building and supplying some of the teachers and church workers. After the new group has grown to thirty, forty, or fifty members they will probably be ready to call a pastor and they will also need a site.

One of the biggest mistakes a new church can make may be in accepting a gift of land for a site. It may be a good piece of land and valuable, but not for the location of a church. So we at the Home Mission Board have a "site fund" and we go in and actually purchase a plot, but here again only after the most careful studies have been made, both of the general area and of the exact location. We take title to the land and hold it for a period of not more than two-and-a-half years, after which the church is usually large enough to take it over and begin paying us back. We also have a Building Fund, and we are ready to lend a church the money with which to build. We know, too, that there may be difficulty in paying the pastor, and we often help to pay his salary *on a decreasing scale* for, let's say, two years. This gives the new church the pastor, a site, and a start on their building.

They then complete their building, hold services, increase their congregation, and grow strong enough to accept the responsibility of every Baptist church which is the sponsoring of another church. By founding a church, by maintaining the evangelical concept, they fulfill their own mission and advance the Gospel.

The Manhattan Baptist Church in New York City has a strange mathematical record. During the past five years that church has added eleven hundred members to its congregation. Yet today the congregation totals only three hundred! The seeming contradiction is in this church's practice of continually sending out its members, volunteers all of them and yet truly missionaries, into surrounding territory to found new churches. The founding members then withdraw from the old church and stay on as a nucleus for the new one. They have started some seven or eight churches in Long Island, Brooklyn, and all over the area. They genuinely know the meaning of going into the next towns to preach the Gospel. This is the basis of *Home* Missions, the realization that here at home, even in a Christian land, there is so much work for a missionary to do. There is no difference in the deep and abiding spiritual needs of people wherever they are, and there is so much to be done in the Blue Ridge Mountains, in the Arizona desert, beside the sequoias of California, and in the heart of the most crowded and bustling borough of New York. Everywhere there are so many who need to be enlisted in active Christian service.

In the Southern Baptist Convention we average the start of two new churches each day—730 new Baptist churches each year. We average baptizing 1,100 persons every day, and this is 400,000 new Baptists in our Convention each year. While this is something accomplished, it is only a glimpse of what is desired, and from our Pioneer Department at the Home Mission Board we are continually sending out missionaries to go into areas where no Baptist work is being done. We also send out Pastoral Missionaries, who have particularly interesting functions. They become pastors of churches in special centers, a college community, a large town, possibly the state capital.

Each of them is actually the pastor of his church, but he is also a missionary to the whole area. His church is the base, his congregation the nucleus, and the pastor and his people are always moving out to start new churches.

There is a Summer Mission Program for young people, and during the summer of 1963 we employed 645 students from colleges, universities, and seminaries each serving for ten weeks in the Program. We paid them twenty-five dollars a week, plus their travel, plus livelihood. We never make it financially attractive enough for them to work only for money, because a part of the plan is for them, and for us, to discover if they are fitted for Christian service. They work with language groups, with Indians, in pioneer fields, at Bible schools, and at revival meetings. They learn, and so do we, who among them are suited for Goodwill Centers serving the underprivileged, who would be particularly valuable at boys' clubs, at parents' conferences, at clinics. We find the girls who should work in kindergartens, in girls' clubs, in clubs for mothers. Because of this experience they are ready to go out as seasoned missionaries just as soon as they have completed their seminary training.

We have about 2,200 Home Missionaries, and this does not count military chaplains. However, there are other kinds of chaplains in ever-increasing numbers, hospital chaplains, institutional chaplains, and industrial chaplains. There is such a continuous demand for chaplains that we maintain a Division of Chaplaincy.

The position of the military chaplain and the official restriction of his duties have given the Home Mission Board an interesting responsibility and privilege. The military chaplain cares for the men actually on the military base, but he does little on the outside. On the outside there are the families of these men, their wives and children. When a camp is started, often near some small town, the little community church cannot possibly care for the families that move in. Sometimes, long after a camp has been activated, there is still a lack of church facilities or at best a crowding of churches and Sunday Schools. So we, usually in co-operation with a State Convention or an Association, may arrange for a ministry to serve these families, and we have found this work to be most rewarding.

Other small churches have similar problems each year when seasonal workers swarm in to gather the crops. We have a Director of Migrant Work, and there is a man in each state to which the migrants travel. The state man goes ahead of the workers, planning with local churches and arranging to meet special needs. We at the Home Mission Board get pretty accurate figures from the government about how many migrants will come to each locality, when they will arrive, and how long they will stay. The local churches then organize their Sunday Schools and prepare their church activities. Of these two million itinerant laborers, eighty-five per cent are outside any church. Here are more than a million-and-a-half men to be worked with, more than a million-and-a-half men who fail to attend any church. Does one need a clearer call? Is the meaning of Home Missions easier to understand?

It may seem strange that in *home* missions we work in both Cuba and Panama. Our work in these countries is part of our language ministry and came about in Cuba because some years ago Spanish-speaking missionaries from Florida traveled over to Cuba and started missions. We have continued the work and today we still have missionaries there, though some of our people have been expelled. There are, however, over a hundred of our Cuban Baptists who are still acting as missionaries so far as we can learn. A few of our churches have been closed, but others are open. We have a seminary and a summer camp.

Our activities in Cuba are limited now compared to what they were, but they still go on. In Panama we started mission work in the Canal Zone at the time of the building of the Canal; it spread and we have continued it.

How does the Home Mission Board carry on its work? Where does it get its money? The Southern Baptist Convention supplies us with a sum each year which comes from the Cooperative Program. This Program is the lifeline of most of our agencies, and it contributes largely to the operation and to the capital needs of the Home Mission Board. Another source of financial support is the Women's Missionary Union, which has a week of prayer each year. During this week they take a special offering for Home Missions. They also have one for Foreign Missions and one for State Missions. Ours is called the Annie Armstrong Offering. Annie Armstrong was one of the early sponsors of Home Missions back at the beginning of the work. She raised money for it and today the offering is named for her.

We receive from that fund approximately three million dollars a year for current operation and mission building. Our total operating budget for 1963 was $5,250,000. We try to make it go as far as we can, and in this chapter I have told you some of the ways—not all—in which we use it.

Missions is really a matter of people; there is no geography in it. An unsaved man at the end of the earth or in the next town is the same in the evangelical concept. Place is insignificant; purpose is all that counts; and in purpose we Baptists are joined. In all missions we are thinking of people—beyond the seas, beyond the hill—and thinking always of salvation and baptism and Christian service.

# *Their Foreign Missions*

John E. Skoglund
Chairman, Foreign Mission Board
American Baptist Convention

Missionaries home on leave from far-off places used to be romantic centers of attraction, bringing an aura of daring and glamour and even a trace of mystery. This did not lessen our understanding of their great service in distant places to men and to God, or cheapen their dedication; it rather added a bit of color and fascination to them and their travels. Mother made her entrance before the assembled family and friends teetering on little wooden shoes, ivory combs in her hair, and her bright kimono bound with a wide and brilliantly colored sash. Father's kimono was of black silk and he quivered a small fan before his face. The daughters were as bright and gay as autumn leaves before a breeze; they might almost have been the "three little maids" from *The Mikado*. It was all fun and all fine because these people *had* been to far-off places and they had a wonderful story to tell that everybody wanted to

*Note:* In this chapter I have used some material from articles written by me at various times for *Missions*.

hear—about the kind of life they lived; the people with whom they associated; the Christian work they were doing in churches, in schools, in hospitals, all of it in those strange places so far away.

Today, if missionaries dressed up like this for an occasion they might hear some lady comment that the wife's kimono was just like the one her husband sent her the last time he was in Japan on duty with the Air Force. Or some man would remark that those wooden shoes surely were hard to walk on; but he had found out a couple of months ago, when he was in Japan selling cotton, that they were mighty handy to use in the muddy streets. And if a little girl on the sidelines said she wanted one of those ivory things for her hair, her uncle would promise to buy her one next week when he was in Tokyo for a meeting of Rotary International.

World War II scattered thousands of American military men and women throughout the Far East, and, at the end of the fighting, they brought the Orient home to us. Japan, China, India turned out to be just over there, not far. The Pacific narrowed until names we had never heard of—Okinawa and Kwajalein, Port Moresby and Sydney—became islands and lands where our people had been. Then the big jets began their streaking and we went to see for ourselves.

The old barriers were blasted away and distance was shortened, but this was the lesser work of war. Nations had been shattered and new nations born of the fragments, but even the making of nations was the lesser work of war. It was in the minds of men where war left its most compelling mark. Colonialism was broken and discarded. Nationalism began its undirected tramplings. The hammer blows of communism sounded their destruction, and the Bamboo Curtain of China wrapped itself around that country shutting off the land and its people. Africa, for so long brooding and silent, now began its stirrings, announcing its claims and demanding to be heard. With the casting out of Western nations from parts of Asia and Africa, the expropriation of American property in various parts of the world, the dismissal of American and European employees from foreign governmental positions, and the actual barring of Westerners from some countries—with all this going on, how could we Americans imagine that our work in foreign missions would be unaffected?

Of course our work has been altered, *but in its outward form only*. The basic thrust of the mission movement itself has not been changed. It continues eternal, rooted in the eternal gospel, for Paul still says to us as he did to the Corinthians: ". . . God was in Christ, reconciling the world unto himself, . . . and hath committed unto us the word of reconciliation. Now then we are ambassadors for Christ, as though God did beseech you by us . . ."

While our purpose continues unwavering, the work of our Christian mission has been drastically affected by the revolutionary forces which have so radically changed life in many areas of the world. Come with me, for example, back to the fall of 1953 when I rode in a jeep ably driven by Missionary Maxwell Chance up the winding steep road from the Assam plains in Northeast India into the Naga Hills. When we reached Kohima, the government administrative center for the Hills, the gates were closed to us. We were politely told that we could not enter. The Naga movement for independence had already begun. Word was sent into the town and soon the Reverend and Mrs. Bengt Anderson, missionaries to the Nagas, came to the gate with a basket and we enjoyed afternoon coffee in a rest house outside the gate.

The Andersons represented the last missionaries in those Hills and soon they too were forced to leave. Thus, for the first time since 1872, when the Reverend E. W. Clark risked his neck to go among the head-hunting Nagas, the Naga Hills had no missionaries and none has been given permission to reside there since 1954.

In that year, 1954, some prophesied that without missionary leadership Christian work among the Nagas would collapse. What actually happened? Church membership has grown more than ten per cent each year. Among the Ao Nagas the average amount given to the work of the church is better than *twenty-five per cent* of a church member's income. At a recent Ao Association meeting a plan for church extension was worked out whereby every unevangelized area would be entered by a representative of the Ao churches.

Each of these churches was asked to release its pastor for one month. During that month the pastors were to go out in teams of two to the non-Christian villages to teach and preach. The people who became Christians during the month would form the nucleus of a Christian congregation in their village. Four months later the pastors were to be released again and would return for further preaching and pastoral work among the newly formed Christian groups. Many of these pastors were laymen with no professional training, but they had been appointed by their churches to perform pastoral duties

This is church extension Naga style. What does it say to us? Clearly we see here a group of people who are primitive in many ways but who have caught the true meaning of God's mission to the world. They understand that the chief task of the church is to witness to the redemption which has come in Christ. In their giving of what they have, and in their going out to give, they exercise this duty as true Christian stewards and witnesses. They have shown that in spite of almost continuous warfare—resulting in the burning of villages, the killing of people, and the disruption of economic life—the Gospel can still be preached and the church extended.

Let us now go out of Assam, out of the Hills, and across the border into Burma where the administration of a large part of the Baptist work for years rested in the Missionary Conference and its Reference Committee. The Burma Baptist Convention met from time to time for fellowship and inspiration only. Today—well, today all that has changed so completely that now the Burma Baptist Convention co-ordinates *all* the Baptist work in Burma. It plans and directs the programs, draws up the budget, handles the funds, requests and assigns missionaries coming from overseas, recruits national workers, and has established the holding body for property formerly held by the American Baptist Foreign Mission Societies. Included within this Burmese membership are various language and area organizations, which themselves have their own programs, planned and administered by their own leaders.

In evangelism, education, scholarships, hospitals, agricultural programs, and the production of literature and audio-visual teaching, the Burma Baptist Convention today plans and carries forward a larger work than ever was known in the heyday of the missionary in Burma. Moreover, there is now only a handful of missionaries on duty in Burma to assist the Convention in its work.

The work of the Nagas and the Burmese illustrates what is happening in every area in which our Foreign Mission Societies are working. No longer is the missionary (or the Mission Board) in the driver's seat. Direction, control, administration—call it what you will—has been taken over by the national church bodies.

Furthermore missions are no longer paid for solely by Americans. In Burma eighty-five per cent of the 1,800 churches are self-supporting. More than five hundred schools, with over fifty thousand pupils, all formerly related to the missions, now are operated entirely as to staff and budget by the national leaders. A sizeable part of the income needed in the work of the Burma Baptist Convention is raised from local sources.

In Assam, every Garo church—and there are 640 of them—is not only self-supporting but also contributes to the work of the Garo Convention and the Council of Baptist Churches in Assam.

In Japan the postwar churches were built on a fifty-fifty basis between the churches and the mission.

In the Philippines, where nearly every church was destroyed in World War II, the Philippine churches themselves bought the land and the equipment and they put up the walls. The Mission Board helped by providing cement floors and galvanized roofs to insure permanence to the buildings.

These conventions not only receive, they send. Almost from the beginning, the Burma Convention has had its own national missionaries in the Hill areas of Northern Burma and across the boundary in Thailand among the Karens. When American Baptists began work among the Thai Karens in 1951 there were already some thirty churches established by national missionaries from Burma.

The Convention of Philippine Baptist Churches a few years ago launched a mission project among the mountain people in two provinces and established a mission station on one of the neighboring islands.

The Japan Baptist Convention is responsible for the oldest Protestant work in Okinawa. It was started not by American missionaries but by Japanese Baptists. When the Okinawans asked the Japan Baptist Convention for the services of an American missionary, the missionary was sent not directly from the United States but from Japan. The missionary was American, but the sharing was by Japanese Christians with the Christians on Okinawa.

With these changes in administration and operation, and the emergence of the nationals and their proven abilities, is the day of the American missionary over? Do we Baptists of this country have no further responsibilities overseas?

The answer of the churches is unmistakable: the day of the missionary is not over and our responsibilities go on. It is the way only, the method of missions, that has changed in places; the purpose and the prayer have not changed.

No longer does the missionary stand as the self-appointed leader, the director of operations. If he comes in that spirit he is not welcome. He comes when he is called for, and he comes as a friend, a counselor, a colleague; most important, he comes as a servant in the name of the servant, Jesus Christ. Whether he be doctor, teacher, or pastor he will be a servant in whatever capacity he is asked to serve by the national church. In those countries of Asia and Africa that are still open to us the churches today are continuing to ask for missionaries. "But the difference," as Bishop Manikam of India said, "is in the *kind* of missionary." He added that the missionary from overseas today must be willing to push the cart from behind rather than pull it from in front. Another distinguished man of India, Principal D. G. Moses of Hyslop College, also described the kind of missionary that is now wanted: "The kind of missionary that this policy calls for is a man or woman who withdraws without separating, who leads without occupying first place, who gives without making the receiver feel that he is receiving; who continuously slaves without getting tired . . . who has denominational relations but ecumenical loyalty."

With so much mission work being taken over by the nationals, should there be regret on our part? Not at all. Ours should be the pride of a parent who sees his son grow up strong and able to take care of himself. Nor should there be resentment about those countries where the forces of politics and revolution have ejected us. Even here there should be the abiding satisfaction of knowing that what we started will go on.

The work of missionaries and of the churches continues in Russia, in Cuba; and even from China we get enough news to know that in the churches the gospel continues to be preached. Ours should be satisfaction and a gratitude that the national churches have strength and leadership. This is the end toward which missions work. The most joyful day in a missionary's heart is that day when he is no longer needed in a place where he has been working, when other leaders have been trained, when churches have been established, when schools are flourishing, so that the roots of the Christian gospel are firmly implanted in the soil of the country and nothing that might come can tear them out. He is free then to move on to another as yet unevangelized place or to give himself to the church as a "partner in obedience."

Once I sat with the executive committee of the Council of Baptist Churches in Assam. One of the first questions that came up was how can we be a mission? All through the years, they said, we have received and now we must give. But what shall we do? Where shall we go? Then a young teacher named Longri Ao at the Theological Seminary stood up and said that he remembered up in the Hills where he had been born there was a whole tribe of people and among them were very few Christians. He knew only five that he himself had baptized when he was in that area preaching some years before. He was talking about the Konyak Nagas, a primitive, opium-smoking, head-hunting tribe. These were the people, he said, to whom they should send a missionary. But who would go? They asked and they asked again, until at last they turned to Longri for his counsel. He stood up once more and he said: "Well, I started this and I guess I'll have to see it through."

Soon thereafter he and his wife and their four children rode the railroad to its end and then, with their packs on their backs, they began the climb into the hills.

Fifty miles they walked until they came into the country of the Konyaks. At the chief village they sought permission to build a house, but the prince of the area said no, we don't want you. You disrupt our native religion. He told them that they could live two miles outside the village, and so they went there. They built a house of bamboo and thatch, and the first year a typhoon blew down the house and the tigers ate up their goats and chickens. It was hard to reach the people, for all day they worked in their scattered fields; but at night, after they had come back from the fields, they would sit in the long house and smoke their opium pipes before a fire. There Longri would go to them and sit with them and talk about Christianity, about the love of God in Christ.

When he began his work a few years ago there were five Christians that he knew of in that tribe. Today there are more than eight thousand. There is a church in every village. This was done, we must remember, without the help of a Western missionary. It was solely the work of the nationals; and I could repeat over and over, in place after place, similar stories of this kind of event in the hills of Assam, Burma, the Philippines, the Congo, and a score of other places.

With such as this confronting us the question comes again: What of the American missionary? What is there for him to do? The answer is not difficult. Whatever has been done, and is being done, is only a beginning. The immediate answer for each individual missionary may not always be clear, for clouds of uncertainty shadow the world and who can make plans for a decade, or a year, or even a month? Yet there is one thing of which we *can* be certain: we stand at the end of an age and we cannot look back. It is never very pleasant to be chased from well-walked and familiar paths toward the jungle of tomorrow, but it is before a tangle that we stand. The gates of yesterday are creaking shut, and we face the future without certainty as to where we are going. We still meet, as before, under the banner of the Foreign Mission Societies; but the day of "foreign missions," as we have known them for one hundred and fifty years, is finished. We had better face up to that fact; or else we shall be left leaning against the gates of yesterday and wishing that somehow they would open again so that we might take our rest among the glories of the past, reciting to an ever-diminishing audience our old and amazing achievements.

The call today is not to rest, not to look back, never to seek comfort in what we have done. The way is ahead and the goals are out yonder. But how—specifically how—can the missionary of today carry out his mission? To begin with there are still a great many carts to be *pushed* by the right kind of missionary working in areas where the nationals have already proved their dedication and abilities. Rest assured that the calls from these churches will not lessen. They will conceivably be even greater, as the work of the nationals expands and the need for missionaries as *associates* increases.

Nor is there any question about this need. For all that has been done in Burma and Thailand, only two per cent of the people there are Christian. Only five per cent of India's population are Christian, and less than one per cent of Japan's and the Arab world. Vast populations in other parts of the world are exploding, and yet they are almost totally un-Christian. There are almost endless areas where missionaries have not been, and it is our continuing responsibility and purpose that we go there, wherever it may be, because the command is clear: Go ye to *all* nations and teach the Gospel. There is no end to missions, either places to go or people to be taught, and there should never be a weakening of the call to individual missionaries.

But how, a young person may ask, do I go about becoming

a missionary? I may have this longing, this call as you say, but what are the requirements? What must I do?

Many of the missionaries we train would come, I suppose, from making some kind of commitment during their high-school course. A great many young people who attend assemblies, summer camps or conventions hear a missionary or a national from abroad; they listen to a personnel secretary from the Mission Board; and this starts the wheels moving in their heads and hearts so that they may sign a card indicating their interest. In the offices of the American Baptist Foreign Missions Society in Valley Forge, Pennsylvania, there are almost ten thousand of these cards that young people have signed. Even larger numbers are on file at the Southern Baptist Board in Richmond, Virginia.

This means that they have made an inquiry and have expressed an interest in mission work. They have not necessarily committed themselves, but they have at least opened the door. So they begin to get some literature and the Personnel Secretary of the Foreign Mission Board may make some suggestions to them about their college courses. He may suggest that anything they do in languages is always good, as well as sociology, history, philosophy. Such studies are particularly needed by the general missionary. They would be useful, too, for men going into medicine and teaching, though these men would naturally soon begin thinking in terms of their own specialty. When they have finished college or university each then goes on to graduate study. Of course, there is a great deal of falling away before the final commitment comes; but those who stay with it will go to graduate school, usually theological or medical. It should be understood that even the doctors and teachers have some time at a seminary to be trained in theology.

Perhaps here is as good a place as any to clarify certain terms that are used in speaking of missionaries. Some Boards speak of "evangelistic" missionaries in distinction from teaching or medical missionaries. Other Boards prefer "general" missionaries, because we feel that in a sense all missionaries, whatever they are doing, are concerned with communicating the Gospel. One need not necessarily preach in order to communicate the Gospel; there are so many other ways to show and teach its meaning.

By the time a young person has gone through graduate school he has generally made his decision to become a missionary. He then must pass intensive health and psychiatric examinations, not only psychiatric tests but also very serious and sometimes prolonged consultations with psychiatrists. The candidate is then ready for presentation to the Personnel Committee, and to them he makes a statement of his Christian commitment and of his concern for missionary service, his "call" as we sometimes speak of it. Out of all this there may come a feeling on the part of the young person that he would like to go to the Congo or to India or to somewhere else in particular. This is more often true than not, but he is also asked to indicate whether he would serve in any field. This is very necessary in the kind of mobile world in which we are living. Western people are sometimes being eliminated from some countries, as in the case of China, and this could happen elsewhere after a young man or woman had been assigned. Then they would *have* to shift.

The physical shifting, however, might mean a good deal less to him than other changes he could be called on to make. He might go out with the idea not only of preaching Christianity but also of extoling his own denomination. In this he would come face to face with one of the greatest issues of mission churches today. Shall the mission of a particular church be a *Christian* mission to the world or a *denominational* mission?

The nationals are the ones who are pressing for Christian

unity. They are saying: we don't want your Western denominational differences. We want Christ and we want a church, but we want it to be our own "indigenous" church. We might possibly want it even to take its coloring and pattern from the culture of the community where the church is. This is very important to us because, after all, Jesus Christ is not a Western Jesus Christ. Christ was here in India, in Burma, in the Philippines, in Japan long before any missionary came. He is the Lord of the World, and he must live in the garment, the dress, and the culture of every people. This question of church and churches the young missionary must face, as the whole missionary world must face it.

There are, as I have been trying to say, many and important changes awaiting the missionary of today, and he will find little of what his grandfather told him. His father's recollections, too, will be misleading. But variance can be growth, and the young man need have no doubt. These are the lesser things that he sees. The eternal things raise no questions and they do not vary.

So now we come to the heart of the whole matter. The mission of the church is not dependent upon our desire to have a better world, or to bring people of other cultures some of the benefits of our culture, or even the noble desire to share with them the best that we have in medicine, education, agriculture, or science. The living, eternal heart of the church's mission lies in the mighty act of God in Christ, in which God takes the initiative to break down all barriers and cross over into the foreign lands of sin and death to make his love known. This is the mission movement, endless, forever in the act of God, and forever in the hearts and lives and work of men.

# *Religious Education in Baptist Churches*

James L. Sullivan
Executive Secretary-Treasurer
The Sunday School Board
Southern Baptist Convention

Sometimes in industry, in sports, in church activities nothing at all seems to happen in some particular area for a long time, then all of a sudden the same thing is happening everywhere. Throughout history there was no automobile. Then Henry Ford took his famous ride and in no time people were seeing weird contraptions of all kinds chugging along the dusty roads. Since the beginning of keeping athletic records nobody had ever run a mile under four minutes. Then, not long ago, one man did it, and right away, so it seemed, half-a-dozen others had done it.

So it was with the Sunday School. Just when and where the first Sunday School was started nobody can say for sure, but a man named Robert Raikes, a printer and publisher of Gloucester, England, gets credit for being "the father of the Sunday School movement." Back in 1780 Raikes saw some children working in a pin factory, unschooled and certainly without moral teaching, and he felt the responsibility of giving them some guidance, so he began teaching them the Bible on Sunday afternoon. He had no sooner started this teaching than Sunday Schools were springing up all over England and throughout the United States.

Actually there may have been Sunday Bible teaching of one kind or another in the American colonies before Raikes, but the Colonial claim cannot be substantiated and the tradition is to give Raikes the credit. Anyway, before the century was out there were many Sunday Schools in England and in this country. The need had always been there, and once the answer was found the spread was rapid and general.

The Bible was the textbook in the first American Sunday Schools, and each teacher expounded whatever passage interested him on any Sunday. There was no plan of any kind in the teaching, and children and grown people often sat side by side. This kept up until the teachers realized that they must have help, and they began asking for special teaching materials. Various organizations answered the request by publishing tracts, pamphlets, and lessons. Finally, with the continuing growth of Sunday Schools in the South and the increasing need for teaching assistance, the Southern Baptist Convention created the Sunday School Board in 1891 and entrusted to it the publication of the necessary materials.

The story of the Board itself is interesting, but more meaningful in our account here is that the present educational program of the Baptist churches had its beginning in this Sunday School movement. I would like to tell the full story of the Board from its picturesque beginning to its present magnitude, but in this chapter we are primarily concerned with religious education in Baptist churches, with something of the philosophy of this education and of its programs.

In our philosophy of education we Baptists are quite different from a church that has a hierarchical structure, because with us everything tends to put emphasis on the individual. This is not only our philosophy but our practice, and all our educational programs are built to protect the individual in his own inherent right of decision, to teach him to think for himself. Our purpose is never to drill information into him so that he will simply give it back to us or to some pastor or to anyone in an unthinking repetition. Baptist education is meant to train a person to be independent in his thinking, to take time to make his own analysis, and to arrive at a decision that is satisfying to him. This is one of the reasons why we want small classes in Sunday School, a teacher whenever possible for each ten younger pupils, and a teacher for not more than twenty adults. This is to give the individual as much chance as possible to develop in his own way according to his own nature and need.

At the same time we want to teach the individual to yield to the vote of the majority in any democratic situation and try never to be childish when he is in the minority group. We urge that he learn to co-operate except when co-operation would be a violation of conscience, and then he will stand unyielding for however long his conscience tells him to. Our plan of education is entirely different from that of any church that does not have this system of individual deliberation and decision and of majority control in each local church.

We want each person to respect the Bible and to love it, a respect and love that he will learn and develop for himself. We do not try to say to any man: "Now, you sit still and be still while I instill." That may be one system of education, but certainly it is not the Baptist way. We attempt to teach a person to be always independent, forever searching and deciding for himself, with his own Bible open before him to guide him.

Our belief in the freedom of the individual, and in the responsibility of the individual, leads us to respect him and to respect his decision, even though that decision may have been born in disagreement with our own and continues to be so in unyielding discussion. Such belief and such practice is the basis of intellectual debate, but at the same time it can be an enduring bond of spiritual union. We Baptists have found it so, and believe completely that within freedom there is union.

In the teaching of these and all other beliefs, the Baptist churches call on the Sunday School Board for multiple aids and supplies; meeting this demand has now become a huge undertaking. Besides the thirty-five thousand churches in the Southern Baptist Convention there are some fifteen thousand other churches in all parts of the world that use our teaching materials. This growth of educational activities has led the Sunday School Board into a number of teaching and training programs.

At this point I would like to remind you of something and make it very clear. The Sunday School Board was created by the Southern Baptist Convention and is a "servant of the churches." The work of the Board, therefore, has its significance in the work of the churches. Our purpose is to provide the churches with publications and other teaching materials and to aid them however we can in their educational activities. The programs that I shall mention may seem to be centered in the Board, but actually they are designed and intended entirely for use by local Baptist churches.

In the first of these programs, in publishing, the Board provides supplies and educational materials to the churches. They include lesson help for both pupil and teacher in the Sunday Schools. They include magazines for church workers to use as promotional and guidance aids. There are papers and magazines to teach character building and to help one grow as a Christian. There are tracts of several kinds, some for promotion of Sunday School, Training Union, and other educational work; still other tracts are to teach doctrine and are designed to be evangelistic. We also publish books to be used as study course textbooks; in leadership training; and to educate Christians in faith, doctrine, moral living, and service. There are general books, too, whose purpose is to help interpret or to guide or to inspire.

We are also concerned with the development of an over-all educational program for the churches, particularly one that is adaptable to churches of all sizes. We want it to be a program versatile enough to be carried out under the direction either of a Minister of Education or by volunteer workers, one that will be helpful to all members whatever their cultural and spiritual backgrounds and whatever their ability to learn and progress. This involves us in the development of various educational concepts, of numerous teaching ideas and their projection. It involves us in the setting of learning goals, administrative procedures, and a search for sound training methods. Nor can this be left to theory only; to implement it calls for field promotion; for the conducting of workshops, conferences, and training schools.

To translate the general purpose and planning of the Board into specific undertakings would itself require a book rather than just a chapter. In fact, these undertakings are so many that I can only list some of them: the Baptist Student Unions on many campuses of the country; Vocational Guidance for young people; Family Life teaching for Christian homes; programs in Church Music, Church Administration, Church Libraries, Church Recreation; and the two big summer Assemblies, one at Ridgecrest, North Carolina, and the other at Glorieta, New Mexico.

To indicate further the variety and extent of our educational programs today I should tell you that the Sunday School Board has a Department of Church Architecture! We Baptists believe in Sunday School departments according to ages, with classes of small numbers; and this kind of teaching cannot be accomplished unless the building is suited to it. As the churches adopt our plan they have to change old buildings or design new ones, and they come to us for help. Today, a whole floor of architects, engineers, and draftsmen help thousands of churches over the world design their buildings.

One of the most rewarding programs of the churches is the Training Union, which was started for training in church membership. Pastors are trained; Ministers of Education are trained; why not church members? They, too, have their responsibilities, and the purpose of the Training Union is to deepen the spiritual lives of church members. It is to help them gain a better understanding of the Bible, a better knowledge of the doctrines of Baptist faith, and to develop attitudes and habits needed for effective participation in the organized life of their church and their denomination. The Training Union has another purpose: to help members develop as Christian citizens, and to help them into a Christian insight of the world situation and a desire to work to improve it.

These educational programs of the churches are our primary concern in this chapter, but I think we might also be interested in a very brief report on the Sunday School Board itself. Actually, such a report will not only tell of the Board's vast growth but will also indicate the educational growth within the Baptist churches, because it is the churches themselves that buy the Board's publications and other materials in millions of copies to be used by them in their religious teaching and training.

Therefore what of the Board today? I mentioned its beginning in 1891, but what of it now? I do not like to cite statistics, measurements, and amounts of money, but I believe I have no other way to tell of the Board's growth and at the same time indicate the growth of the educational programs in our churches.

The Sunday School Board began with one man and one desk in a room corner that was borrowed from some friends. The man's wife had inherited five thousand dollars and she loaned it to him. This was all he had, in equipment and money, for six months.

Today the Board is housed in a twelve-story building with a seven-story building beside it and a six-story building across the street. There is also an operational building that is three blocks long; you could put five football fields on top of it. The original desk space has now become some twenty acres of floor space in Nashville alone! And the five thousand dollars would now last about twenty minutes, for the operational budget of the Board approaches one hundred thousand dollars every working day, about thirty million dollars a year.

An even more interesting fact, perhaps, is that all these costs are met by the income of two programs: Publishing and the forty-seven Baptist Book Stores that are scattered over the country to distribute our teaching materials and supplies. This income not only pays all costs, improvements, and reserves, but leaves enough over for us to help in various education and service programs.

In the present century the little red school-house has just about disappeared, and in its place are the large city and county schools leading on through the whole system of secular education to the complex of the great universities. The churches have made comparable progress in their Christian education, extending their teaching into the homes and onto the campuses; making use of Sunday Schools and Training Unions; making use of libraries, music, church administration, and vast use of publications. The sermon on Sunday morning is the center of the church's teaching, but there are also numerous other approaches to members through Christian teaching and training throughout the week.

And what do I mean when I speak of Christian teaching and Christian education? I mean all the things that a person should know morally, ethically, and spiritually to make him a full person, a whole person. This is the objective of Christian teaching, and this is the substance of Christian education. This is our objective in printing a Sunday School lesson or a book. This is why there is a Baptist Student Union and a Training Union. This is the objective of the church in all its various forms of education. The constant purpose of Christian education is that a person shall become a whole person in Jesus Christ.

# The Christian Campus

Andrew B. Martin
President
Ottawa University

Scattered over the country, most often on neat and shady campuses, in little towns or in cities, are any number of small colleges. If one should look closely, say at an archway over the campus entrance or at some quietly lettered sign not far away, one could read the name of the college followed perhaps by: "A denominational institution founded and supported by the __________ denomination." These are the church colleges of the country. The likes of them were started some two centuries ago in America for the instruction of ministers. Harvard was founded in 1638 so as not "to leave an illiterate ministry to the churches, when the present ministers shall lie in the dust." Brown University, originally Rhode Island College, was founded in 1674 by the Baptists, the first Baptist college in the Colonies "to secure for their church an educated ministry."

The continued presence of these colleges prompts a question: Why, with so many state-supported institutions offering education to every man and woman in the state, do we need church colleges?

Furthermore, in church colleges today only a small percentage of students prepare for the ministry or any other church vocation. The Baptist institution at Ottawa, Kansas, which is incorrectly called Ottawa University—it is really a college—can serve, I believe, as a fair example of a present-day liberal arts church college. It is distinctly a Christian college, of the Baptist denomination, and is clearly a church college; yet only ten per cent of our present students are preparing for church service either as ministers or otherwise. This is true—with the percentage varying—of most church colleges today.

So we come back to the question: Why, with state universities and their branches all over the state, do we continue with church colleges?

One reason is that church colleges still fulfill the function for which they were founded: they still prepare *some* men for church vocations (and women, too, nowadays). Moreover, these students are more significant in the over-all training program of the churches than their number, or any percentage, might indicate.

Another reason is that they train laymen for church leadership. The place of the layman is now undergoing a tremendous change, and his importance in the church is being recognized. Our college responsibility is to see that the men and women who leave here not only have an intelligent understanding of Christianity but that they also know how they can best serve as laymen in their churches.

There is a third reason for the church college, not so distinctive perhaps as the other two, or so easy to define, but "the spiritual dimension of life" or "the religious aspect of life" gets a better hearing, I believe, in a church college than in a non-church institution. Teachers at church colleges do not hesitate to face religious issues in the classroom and discuss them. Questions concerning religion, the ultimate questions of our lives, are handled openly and fully, and perhaps this is one reason why students, even those with no thought of a church vocation, still seek out the church college; they like the character of the place. Of course, one should say that any fine teacher, at a state university or wherever he may be, injects philosophy and the great truths into the presentation of his immediate subject; but I believe that this kind of teaching is more likely to occur at a church college.

Another reason for the Christian liberal arts college is its continuing concern for the individual. The intellectual elite are recognized and honored, but the ordinary fellow is given his chance too. I believe that an ordinary man at a church college has more opportunity to show leadership than at an institution less concerned with the individual.

There are other reasons, some rather personal. One woman long out of a church college said that she never felt about another place quite as she did about her college. While she was there the college had been interested in her, and some of her teachers still were interested in what she was doing. Now, in contributing to the college, she felt that she was helping to care for a parent who had done so much for her. This kind of feeling, an intimate and personal loyalty, is found particularly, I think, among church college graduates.

In honesty, we should take into account a possible risk in church colleges. Each of them is of some denomination, and such a college may be so insistent on presenting denominational preachments, so determined to get doctrines into its instruction, that the general educational level may suffer. This practice is not common, but it should be mentioned.

The usual plan is to present denominational teaching only in denominational subjects. We do not insist on operating simply as a Baptist college at Ottawa. We invite young people of all denominations, and we have people of different churches on our faculty. We prefer to think in terms of a Christian college—the Christian point of view, the Christian conviction, the Christian approach to life—rather than strictly the Baptist outlook.

All our courses on Baptist subjects are optional. We recommend them to people going into the ministry or missionary service or any church vocation, but we do not require even ministerial students to major in religion. Instead, we urge ministerial students to get as much of the liberal arts as possible and leave their strictly professional training to the seminary. Of course the Baptist influence is here, just as the Christian influence is here, but we are primarily and distinctly a *college*.

Now we come to something that is puzzling. Despite high standards in church schools and some very distinctive advantages, the total enrollment at these colleges, when compared to enrollment at state institutions, is decreasing. Not so long ago more than fifty per cent of the total college enrollment of the country was in church colleges. Today their national percentage is down to forty per cent, thirty-five per cent.

Why is this? When one totals up tuition, fees, and living expenses, there is little difference, if any, in the over-all cost at most state universities and most church colleges. There is often no appreciable difference in distance. Why, then, are an increasing percentage of young people choosing the state institution over the church college?

I wonder if it isn't partly because some young people today may lack an understanding of why they go to college. Uncertain about it, they set up standards of their own and go to the state university because sometimes it is easier to get admitted there. They go, too, because they are already thinking about a job, and they can get more vocational or professional training at a state university where there are schools of journalism and schools of design. They also have in mind that maybe they can make some professional connections that might pay off later. At state universities there are bigger fraternities and bigger sororities and bigger houses, and some church colleges do not have fraternities at all. There are more famous football teams and bigger celebrations at state universities. All this can lead to exciting experiences for young people, but when it comes to education and learning and preparing to live, such experience is misleading and often meaningless.

What really is an educated man? He is one who, somewhere along the way, has realized that his mind is very important and he has learned how to use it. What is more, he *is* using it. This is education's plan of bringing an intelligent outlook to all aspects of a man's life.

It is possible that a young person, though markedly intelligent, may still be uncertain about what he is doing and quite insecure in his plan for living. The function of the Christian college, beyond any teaching and development of learning, is to give all young persons a greater spiritual maturity. It is the responsibility of the college, and those associated with it, to see that young people have a new and more penetrating understanding of what they have been taught, a new surety in what they are doing, and a greater confidence in themselves and their eternal future. This is the duty and the privilege of the Christian college over and above all else, and I do not think there is anything more important than implanting intelligence and faith in the lives of young people.

We do not always succeed, and there are young persons at church colleges and every institution of learning, who are there primarily to get a degree because of what it will do for them later on—its market value. And they want to get it for the least they can give. Students are attending lectures, taking down notes, and giving back on the examinations what they think will will please the professor, and nothing more. This is not intellectual activity or education; it is a form of regurgitation, and it is happening all over the country. Finally, when the course is over, they close the book and it is finished. I went to graduate school with a fellow and we used to walk home together. Almost invariably when we came out of a class he would say: "Well, Martin, that's another one sawed off." He was sawing wood, just sawing it off a log at a time.

What every really intelligent teacher wants to see happen is an awakening within a student. In my own mind there is an interesting connection between an intellectual awakening and a religious conversion. Religion, to the person who has not been converted, is an unknown world. He hears people talk about it but he does not quite get involved. Then at some time in his life he may come to a kind of crisis, and he awakens to the fact that there is another dimension of life, one that he has known nothing about up to this time. This is what I think real conversion is. Something actually happens to a man.

This is what happens when a student awakens to the fact that the whole world of knowledge is continuously fascinating and sometimes breath-taking—*and that he can get involved in it!* Then no more does he say: "How many words do you want, Professor?" He says: "I'll be reading this next time. And *this* next. I'll write you a paper on it. I'd like to get to the bottom of it." This is an intellectual awakening, a conversion within the mind.

I remember a young Filipino who studied biology at Ottawa. It did not mean a thing to him. He was untouched by it, as most of the other students were. Then one day he was working in the laboratory with a microscope. He kept looking, and I do not know what he saw that day, but at the end of the period he went to the teacher and asked: "Would you mind if I came back and worked on this in my spare time?" Before he left us he said he was going to make biology his life work. He went on to graduate school and now is back in the Philippines, a professor of biology. As I say, I don't know what he saw in the microscope that day any more than I know what other men see when they have visions and begin to dream dreams.

If education means to students simply that they get a degree and close the books they have no conception of the intelligent life and will never live it. At college they should be getting experience that will open the world to them, so that the mysteries of man are seen and the mysteries of God are worshiped.

Sometimes I believe that we teachers and administrators do not think enough about our part in all this and do not recognize that we, too, may have some conceptions that are awry. It is quite possible that we mumble too many rules and regulations and shape too many patterns to which students must conform. We create too many molds for them to fit into. We ought to be thinking about the young fellow who is coming along the hall to keep an appointment with us, and how we can get him going with his own intellectual and spiritual power so that when he leaves the college he will keep going.

# *Their Publications*

Glenn H. Asquith
Executive Director
Division of Christian Publications
American Baptist Convention

Sometimes an invention, such as Gutenberg's invention of movable type, can jar history and send her hurtling down a new path, sweeping the old ways aside. Many times, though, an invention comes quietly, taking history by the hand, leading, content to add new dimensions to paths already found. Perhaps such a quiet invention, a new lamp, played a part in setting the reading habits of an early America and in its way influenced the beginning of our Baptist publications.

Back in 1824 a new lamp had been invented so that people could read after the day's work was done, and an awareness of the printed page was decidedly on the rise in America. Newspapers were coming over from England and others were being started here. Literacy was on the increase; transportation was opening up new areas of the country; democracy was moving across the land; and people wanted information of all kinds. In the midst of this restlessness the secular publishers were turning out their products, and the churches saw an opportunity to deal with the spiritual life of the people. So, in 1824, the faculty and students of Columbian College in Washington, D.C., called for a meeting of the Baptists to organize the Baptist General Tract Society.

The purpose was evangelism by providing tracts for the missionaries who were moving westward over the mountains and across the plains, playing their part in the great migration. The tracts were printed in Philadelphia and were sent out from there on canal barges, steam packets, wagons, stage coaches, and horseback. Some of this material was used directly from the barges and packets, being distributed at various stopping points along the way. Some was dropped at smaller settlements, and there men waited to carry it deeper into the frontier areas well off the lines of travel.

These men proved their zeal in the hardest way, for they were the *colporteurs,* "the neck porters," who walked and carried the tracts and booklets in two baskets that swung at the ends of a yoke held across their shoulders, such a device as one sees today used by porters and farmers in the Orient. Whatever a colporteur could get for his tracts he took, but if the people had no money he would give them away because this, to him, was a part of the general missionary endeavor. It was "the use of the printed word as a means of evangelism," as the Reverend Noah Davis, one of the early great leaders among the Baptists, described it.

Along with the colporteurs other men were traveling on horseback, their saddlebags stuffed with tracts. They rode the backwoods trails until ways were opened that were usable by wagons, and then the horseman took to the wagons because in this way he could carry more tracts. Finally, the railroads pushed on westward into entirely new areas, and then a real missionary innovation came into use. It was the "chapel car."

At one end of this railroad car lived the missionary, taking up perhaps one-quarter of the space, his tracts and booklets packed in boxes and crates around his living area. At the other end was the chapel, with a pulpit and chairs and even an organ and hymn books. The car would be left at some stop along the roadway and the missionary would hold services until the train came along next time, then he would be picked up and carried farther on out. Finally, though, he would come to the end of the line, and there he had an arrangement with the railroad by which the chapel would be left for an indefinite period while he used it as a base, traveling in all directions to pass out his tracts and preach. When he had completed his work in this region he and his car were picked up and taken to some other place where he would begin all over again.

The last of the chapel cars has been saved and it is now on exhibit as a museum piece on the grounds of the American Baptist Assembly at Green Lake, Wisconsin.

This pioneer work was carried on by the original Tract Society until 1844, when the organization was given a new name, The American Baptist Publication Society. The constitution of that year declared it was founded "to promote evangelical religion by means of the Bible, the printing press, colportage, and the Sunday School." This plan of mission work seemed good enough to those who wrote it, but the colporteurs and other distributors of tracts, as they moved deeper into the backwoods, saw a need that they could not fulfill. They began reporting this to Philadelphia and Washington. They said that men were needed to come out and stay, not just preach and travel on.

This report was answered by "area missionaries," who went out to settle in various parts of the frontier. They had hardly arrived, certainly had not finished building their houses, when they saw a prime need. Nothing in the way of Christian teaching was being offered the young people, so the missionaries set about organizing Sabbath schools to meet on Sunday afternoons. These meetings were successful, for the young people came; but in a very short time word was coming back from the missionaries that they had nothing to lead with and nothing to use as a basis for instruction. So the Publication Society in Philadelphia began to develop and print teaching materials. This was done as quickly as possible, but as more Sunday Schools developed, and more missionaries settled along the frontier, some of them pushing out ahead of it, the need for teaching materials increased beyond any anticipation. In fact, the demand grew at such a surprising rate, and the Society had to develop so much of this material, that finally the original tracts became the lesser effort and the writing and printing of curriculum materials the greater one.

Up until the year 1845 the American Baptist Publication Society and its predecessors supplied all the literature used by Baptists in the United States, but in that year there was the separation between the churches in the North and the churches in the South. The Southern churches made their own provisions until the Civil War, but the wholesale destruction and disruption made it impossible for them to continue providing teaching materials, and for twenty years following the Civil War our Society in Philadelphia supplied our sister churches in the South with whatever they needed.

Several Baptist Conventions now have publication programs and we could not possibly describe all of them. Let it be said, though, that each was started to answer needs, never simply as an additional Convention activity. They all, too, have the common purpose of education. Whatever may be their plan of operation, however their materials may be written and published, all their programs are dedicated essentially to Christian education. With this basic purpose in mind we can suggest at least something of the over-all Baptist publication program, even though I am somewhat limited to the program that I know best, since I am a part of it.

There is one endeavor which is the same in each program: the Uniform Lesson. In 1872 a committee appointed by all the evangelical denominations of North America met to plan a sequence of Bible study. Every six years they would complete a study of the entire Bible, and each year they would include some phase of Christ's life. The Lessons still are planned in this way, and they are inter-denominational to the extent that all churches that use them accept the chosen scripture verse, the Memory Verse, and the emphasis of the Lesson. The committee, however, provides only this general material and makes no attempt whatever to offer any interpretation. The interpretation is left to each denomination that accepts the general material, who then write their own Lessons according to their denominational need and doctrinal distinctiveness.

Uniform Lessons were used everywhere until the grade system in the public schools proved its benefits, then some of the teachers in Sunday Schools began asking for graded lessons, which were to be planned for children according to their ages and abilities. They also insisted that children be promoted from year to year in their Bible study, as in their day studies, and that Sunday School teaching be a steady progression just as day school was, moving upward year by year.

The preparation of Graded Lessons in the beginning was an individual effort, but their planning now has developed into an inter-denominational work, with the participating churches again writing and editing to satisfy their denominational requirements. Despite the popularity of the Graded Lessons, the Uniform Lessons hold their own and are the preference of many churches. Both, however, are an important part of our publication program and are constantly being shipped out to the various churches in quantities according to their demands.

The mention of distribution prompts me to interrupt my story for a moment to recall the old colporteurs plodding along the narrow roads and wooded paths, burdened with their neck yokes but with their loads lightened by belief in their mission. Today there is no less faith, I am sure, but modern distribution is made by fleets of huge shining trucks that come to our great building at Valley Forge where our publications are loaded into them. Once they are filled, they head out over the highways and into the same territory traveled by the colporteurs, passing through it and crossing the old frontiers, going all the way West, making their deliveries to our bookstores in Chicago, Los Angeles, Seattle. The present day method of carrying out the mission is dramatically different than before, but its purpose has not changed and the intent still is "the use of the printed word as a means of evangelism."

I have told you that our earliest productions were the tracts, and then in 1841 we timidly started our first story paper, the *Sabbath School Gleaner*. Fifteen years later, in 1856, we acquired the New England Sunday School Union with all its rights and properties, and among these was a youth publication, the *Young Reaper*. We merged the two and together they became *Young People*, which continues today and is our oldest document.

And here again I want to wander a moment. Many of today's adults began reading *Young People* decades earlier, and it continues as a regular part of their reading habit. Not so long ago we took a survey and found that people in their sixties and seventies were reading every issue of *Young People*. We thought this was fine and we were proud of it; then we received a letter from a man who was eighty-one. He complained about *Young People*, saying that it had changed since he began reading it. "Today," he wrote, "you are slanting it too much to young people!" (The exclamation point is ours.)

Our publication program is too extensive even to suggest it in any detail, but besides all the Sunday School materials it includes a great many periodicals, books, and booklets. There are, for instance, Leadership Texts, Vacation Church School Books, Released Time Manuals, Camping Guides, Administration Helps, Missionary and Stewardship Education Texts, and numerous other study guides.

There are attractive quarterlies, making possible an all-family evening fellowship: *Secret Place*, a family devotional quarterly, Braille editions of Primary and Junior lessons, books to guide in church organization and management, twelve to fifteen new volumes annually on a variety of subjects from administration to drama, biographies, Bible studies, and poetry.

The whole program is dynamic. It is never fixed and never ends. We constantly revise, considering each piece to see how it can be improved. We ask our field men what they have heard. What have they seen? What needs have they noted? How can we meet these needs?

We listen to the churches. A pastor of a very small church writes that our camping materials are unsuited to his needs. His letter is promptly taken to the committee on youth work. Every suggestion is examined, for out of these have come some of our best ideas. We are always sensitive to any request from the churches. And why not? That is why we are here: to serve the churches by publishing materials that will be useful to them.

Young people might be interested to know that we have college students on our Board of Managers. This is the Board which considers and decides everything we do, and these young people have a very strong voice in making policy. They are elected from the Baptist Student Movement and the Baptist Youth Fellowship, and they regularly attend the Board meetings, nothing being decided without them.

In 1844 the small forerunner of the American Baptist Convention stated its goal: "To promote evangelical religion by means of the Bible, the printing press, colportage, and the Sunday School." Today the colporteurs are gone, but the great trucks are streaking westward and the original goal remains. We are still here to promote evangelical religion by means of the Bible, and by means of whatever lessons, periodicals, and books we can develop and print for the teaching and the conversion of men.

# They Care When You Are a Child

W. R. Wagoner
General Superintendent
Baptist Children's Homes of North Carolina

The bombed-out cities, burned villages, and deserted farms of World War II were cluttered with more than the wreckage of buildings and houses. Amidst the debris lived children—homeless, hungry, and existing however they could. We saw the same tragedy again at the time of the Korean War. We sent food and packages and some of our soldiers were so moved that they adopted children and brought them home for healthful and decent rearing.

Lost and bewildered children have always been a part of the heritage of war, and it was so following the War Between the States in 1861–1865. Homes and cities had been burned and children were left fatherless, numbers of them without either parent. In North Carolina, as in all Southern states where there had been devastation, many children were without adequate care. The need was plain and the Baptists, among other groups, did what they could to give some kind of help; but these were Reconstruction days, when poverty and hardship lay across the land, and it was not until 1885 that the North Carolina Baptist Orphanage Association opened its first home in Thomasville.

Most of the early homes, regardless of the founding organization, were "orphanages." The children had lost both parents and needed care because of poverty—often extreme poverty and even destitution. This is not true today. Only five per cent of the children now at our home in Thomasville are completely orphaned. Another twenty-nine per cent have lost one parent. This leaves about two-thirds of our children with both their parents living.

Since the thirties, and particularly since World War II, there have been an increasing number of reasons, other than economic need, for children to come to us. There may, of course, have been the physical death of the parents and the children are truly orphans. More likely there have been mental and physical breakdowns in the family. There have been desertions, separations, divorce. Immorality, alcoholism, violation of the law and the imprisonment of a parent have played their part in the breakup of homes. Most of our children are victims of circumstances that they cannot understand and that they resent. This means that they are more difficult to help than the orphaned child.

An orphan can accept death because he can see death, nor does he have to debate it or explain it to himself or to his friends. A child, though, cannot comprehend why his home is unstable or why his parents should be unable or unwilling to care for him, forcing him to go elsewhere to live in strange surroundings and with new people. It is lonely and puzzling for any child and almost impossible for a very young child to understand. Only after he is thirteen, fourteen, fifteen does the average child make up his mind to adjust to his lot—perhaps with a few hidden scars—and to place himself with us, not only physically but emotionally. From then on out we are able to work with him more effectively.

How does a child get to the home in the first place? The probable beginning is with an inquiry from a parent or both parents, a grandparent, an uncle, an aunt. The local Department of Public Welfare or some other agency concerned with the welfare of children may write to us that John and Jane Smith are in need of care. Is there anything that we can do about it?

We begin investigations and usually several months are spent by one of our case workers visiting the home, the pastor, and various people in the community. The worker is trying to determine if the home is hopelessly broken or if there is any way to save it, even to the extent of our providing financial aid to solve some temporary difficulty. If our findings indicate that nothing can be done about the home, then we search for some relative who might make provision for the children. If no suitable home can be found with a relative, we accept responsibility for the children and try to decide what type of care is best suited for them. Children are very different in this respect. One child would do well to come to us here in Thomasville for group living among a number of other children. Another child might not be happy here, and he should be placed in a different kind of care. If he is quite young and has never known a good mother and father he probably should go into a foster home that we select for him.

Once a child comes under our care the case worker does not necessarily give up on the family. He continues trying to re-establish the home, providing of course that the parents are suited to the normal responsibilities of parents. The mother or father may need medical care, or counseling from the pastor, or employment. Getting a child back into his own home is almost always our desire, and this has been more successfully accomplished than one might imagine. Each year we see more and more homes brought together again, with parents once more taking up their rightful responsibilities and children returning to more normal lives.

There are four Baptist homes for children in North Carolina; the oldest is the Mills Home in Thomasville. What about the children who live with us here in group care?

Some homes for children, particularly the orphanage type, of which there are still some, have been inclined through the years to accept children only from four to twelve years. They have always felt it difficult, and in some cases impossible, to bring a child successfully into group care after he has passed twelve. This, however, has changed for the most part because of the increasing needs of older children—thirteen, fourteen, even up to seventeen and eighteen occasionally. We accept more children today in the age group of thirteen-fourteen-fifteen than any other. Because of the prevalence of divorce and the increased number of broken homes we have come to disregard age in accepting our children.

Before a child arrives here, and once our investigations indicate that he is likely to come to us, the case worker begins talking with him, letting him know what lies ahead, trying to get him ready for the separation from his family. We do everything we possibly can during this period, sometimes for months, to make the child ready for the move from his home to group care with us.

When finally he comes, the case worker brings him and stays with him as closely as he can, for the case worker is the one person that the child knows and can hold to. At the same time all of us in the administration—the pastor, the house parents in the cottage where he will live—all of us do our best to ease things for him, to let him know that we recognize him as an individual, as somebody, and that we are happy to have him and that we love him. Sometimes the boy or girl has already visited the campus, has seen the buildings, the church, and has met members of the staff. This helps, of course, but it is the case worker who is the friend and the really stabilizing influence, a go-between for all that is being encountered.

We have nineteen cottages and each one has a house parent, or house parents, for we are increasingly employing husband and wife as a team. They may or may not have children of their own; if they do, their children live in the cottage along with the others and do just as they do. Besides the house parents, each cottage has a dietitian who is responsible for preparing the food and serving the meals. This way is very different from the older practice, still followed in some homes today, where a single large dining room serves for everyone. We much prefer the smaller groups, with children living as near a normal family life as possible.

Here at Mills Home we have room for 306 children and we would like each cottage to have only twelve children or fewer in it; we never allow more than eighteen. The cottages originally were built like barracks, with twenty-five, thirty, even forty children sleeping in each of them. We renovated and converted them to a more intimate scale and we hope to replace them with cottages built for a maximum of twelve children in each.

There is a difference of opinion about how many children should sleep in a room. In some child-caring agencies there are four children to a room; at others three, sometimes two, and even one. I prefer a flexible arrangement because some children get along better with four to a room. Other children should room alone. We try to meet the needs of each child, so far as we can.

One thing more about living arrangements. We are trying to establish a plan by which brothers and sisters can live in the same cottage. Boys would live on one side and girls on the other; brothers and sisters under the same roof, seeing each other at mealtime, at cottage worship, living together as they did in their own homes.

The house parents are responsible for the daily care and keep of the children and for all discipline, except when, occasionally, some problem must be taken to the local superintendent. Several of our children undoubtedly had a tendency to delinquency before coming to us; but when such a child is removed from the damaging environment in his home or neighborhood, when he begins to live in Christian surroundings with Christian people, his difficulties usually lessen and sometimes disappear. We have found that unfortunate surroundings seem to make most delinquents.

One of our prime responsibilities is the health of our children, and we have on campus a well-equipped infirmary with a registered nurse and a practical nurse. A physician is on our payroll, subject to our call day or night, and he makes routine visits to our infirmary just as he visits the hospital in the town. A surgeon is on our staff, and when surgery is needed our children go to the hospital in Thomasville or they go to Winston-Salem or High Point if a specialist is required. We have two dentists on our staff and our children visit them in their offices uptown. Particular attention is paid to the regular health and dental checkup for all the children.

There is a church on the campus and a pastor, and our plan is shaped toward a life that a child would live in a Christian home. There are no binding rules in regard to all religious activities, and the children participate in the Training Union, in mission organizations, and other auxiliary services on a voluntary basis. They all know, however, that they are expected to be in Sunday School each Sunday morning and at Sunday worship services. Then, too, each cottage has its own devotions conducted by the house parents, with the children themselves participating in various ways.

Our children attend five different public schools in Thomasville. We don't want them massed together in one school because they might tend to stay together. There was a time when the Mills Home had its own athletic teams, but this caused friction between our children and the town children and so we ended them. As soon as our boys and girls began playing on the regular teams they soon lost their identity with the Mills Home and became full members of their school communities, fully participating and fully accepted.

Every child in our care has a work assignment. The small children—the first, second, and third-graders—are responsible for keeping their own beds made and their rooms tidy. The older children have more responsibility: helping prepare and serve the food, working with the campus maintenance crew, helping in the recreation program. The boys are taught printing, farming, dairy farming, electrical and mechanical maintenance, carpentry, and other trades. The girls learn sewing, cooking, housekeeping, and, if they wish, they can gain experience in nursing, printing, library and secretarial work.

During the summer the work program continues on the farm, in the dairy, the cottages, the shops; but in this time every child has a vacation when he leaves the home for at least two weeks. He has another vacation for ten days at Christmas. There are also vacations at Easter and Thanksgiving, and any child with an invitation is allowed to leave for several days. Some children have relatives—a father or mother, grandparents or an aunt, perhaps—with whom they can visit, and if these relatives want the child for a long period in the summer he may stay with them. Those children without relatives visit homes where they have been invited and where our case workers know the families. If a child has no invitation, a worker then makes this known, and usually some family will give the boy or girl the happiness of being in a home for a holiday. We think this is very important because it gives the child a chance to see how a Christian family lives and works and they may never have been in such a home before.

Our boys and girls have the privilege of securing work off the campus during the summer before their senior year of high school. The experience gives them some knowledge of the outside working world, eases the impending break from institutional care, and helps them prepare for a permanent job. This summer work is arranged with the help of the case worker, who finds out the kind of work that a boy or girl wants, helps to make application at some plant or business, and takes the young person for interviews and testing. The case worker supervises the summer work, knows its results, and can give better advice in the permanent planning.

When a child finally leaves our care he always has some place to go. We have no provision for those young people who have completed high school, but they are never simply turned loose. We make certain that they have jobs, or are going on to college or into military service. Of course, children sometimes leave us before they finish high school. Things may have changed enough in the family for the parents to want him back, or he may want to go out on his own either to work or to military service. When this happens, and we have determined that there *is* a place for him to go, we wish him well and watch him fondly as he goes.

Merely because a boy or girl has left us does not mean that we forget him. His case worker stays in touch with him for at least a year, and longer if it seems wise. There is no end to our relationship with our children, and some of them, after they have been away five years, ten years, may come back for a brief stay, particularly at some time of stress for them. This is their home and they come back for stability and reassurance.

A good many of our students go on to college, and we help any of them who have the ability and the aspiration. We help them to make application, take them to visit the college if possible, and help them financially. We cannot fully support the student in the college of his choice, but we can help with a scholarship of three, four, or even five hundred dollars. In addition, we have a loan fund from which students can borrow. We encourage them to work during the summer to make money for clothes and other necessities. Also, most of them work from one to three hours a day while they are at college. Then, too, some Baptist of the state will now and then provide a scholarship. We try to enable each of our students, who is capable of a college education and wants it, to achieve their desire. We plan for them to have the best start in life that is possible for them. At present, thirty of our students are in college.

So far we have been discussing only group care. I should now mention foster homes. They are a part of our total program where parents give a Christian home to children who no longer have homes of their own. These foster homes are most carefully selected and must meet the qualifications that are set up by the Children's Homes and the State Department of Public Welfare. Once we are convinced about a home, after visits and inspection, we recommend it to the Department of Public Welfare and they license it. This is a proper safeguard for the child and for all concerned.

No child of pre-school age, six and under, is brought to the Mills Home for group care. Instead, a child so young is always placed in a foster home where he lives as a member of the family and receives close supervision and affectionate care. He will not be adopted by the foster parents and he will keep his own name. There are never more than four children in any one foster home.

Having gone to live in this home when he is quite young, a child may stay there through grammar school and even high school. The time may come, though, when it seems better for him to live with a larger group. Whenever this happens we offer him the chance of coming here to us and living with groups of other children. Every so often just the opposite of this occurs and we see a child living with us who would progress further in a foster home. We discuss the idea with him and, if he wishes, we seek out a home that is suited for him. Wherever a child is, he continues under our care. We pay monthly amounts to each foster home for the care of our children, and our case workers regularly visit them to make sure that all is well.

Besides the foster homes that we use, we have the home for group care here in Thomasville, another in Kinston, a third in Pembroke, and I would like to mention in particular a new home that we have recently opened in Chapel Hill. This latest home is for our emotionally disturbed children. A number of our children suffered emotional damage before coming to us and we have reguarly taken them back and forth to Chapel Hill where they received psychiatric treatment as out patients. This was not adequate for a few of the children, and so we have opened a cottage in Chapel Hill where these children live, attend school, enjoy normal lives, and receive continuing treatment at the Department of Psychiatry of the University Medical School. The cottage in Chapel Hill has its house parents, its dietitian, and all our usual care; it might perfectly well be on our campus in Thomasville except for the treatment received by the children. The other children who had been receiving psychiatric attention, those who live with us and who need less intensive treatment, are still regularly taken to Chapel Hill as out patients.

Few of the families of our children can contribute anything toward their support. The ability to pay is studied at the time of application and the case worker reports on it. There may be a father or a mother, a grandparent or some relative who could make a small monthly contribution, and, whenever there is, we ask that this be done. It ties the relative closer to the child and also somewhat helps our situation here. Actually, though, the amount contributed by relatives is very small, a total of less than two per cent of our income.

We have four primary sources of income. The Cooperative Program of our North Carolina Baptist Convention provides thirty-three per cent. Each year at Thanksgiving a special offering for the Children's Homes is given by the churches; it provides thirty per cent. Many churches still have what they call Once-a-Month-Offerings, and these offerings provide sixteen per cent. All other sources—payments by relatives, Social Security, Veterans benefits, income from endowment, and miscellaneous income—accounts for twenty-one per cent. This makes our total, and if in any year the offerings happen to be light we just tighten our belts and go ahead. We always manage.

We should say something about the philosophy of our child-care program. In the first place we try to make the whole program as solidly Christian as we can. As a part of this, and as a bedrock Baptist principle, we recognize every child as significant in the sight of man and sacred in the sight of God.

There is not much that we can do about a child's background, but there is something that we can do about what lies ahead and the direction in which he will go. Our plan is in the education of the child, in his rehabilitation and conservation; it is a ministry of missions, evangelism, love, and affection. We can provide clothing, food, shelter, but we try to go far beyond this to a ministry of Christian teaching and redemption.

Many of the children we serve have been let down, disappointed by adults, and they have lost faith in grown-ups. They have lost faith in themselves. They have lost faith in God. We take every child as he comes to us and we try to rebuild in him the faith that he has lost, letting him know that somebody cares for him, that there is love and affection to be shared with him. No matter what has gone before he can square his shoulders, look the world in the face, be grateful for being alive and for being himself. He can take advantage of all the opportunities immediately around him and have confidence about what lies ahead. He has the right to work and the privilege to worship, and no other man has any more.

# They Tend the Sick

T. Sloane Guy, Jr.
Executive Secretary-Treasurer
Southern Baptist Hospital Board

Most things come about for one of two reasons, human needs or human desire, and oftentimes a combination of the two. Certainly the best in our civilization has risen when human need was answered by a consecrated desire to do something about it. Such was the case in the establishment of hospitals.

The first hospitals were at the time of the Crusades some eight or nine hundred years ago, when men began caring for the sick, the wounded, and the drop outs on the long marches. A "hospital" was a room, a tent, a wayside station of any kind, where the helpless could be gotten out of the weather and given some food and water.

For hundreds of years after this in Europe the story of hospitals was mostly a shameful one. They were little more than dumping grounds for the sick, the insane, the feeble of all kinds jumbled in together and left to live or die with little attention. Charles Dickens wrote about the horror of these places, and our word *bedlam* grew from the name of one of them because of its uproar and wild confusion.

Gradually, though, kindness and decency asserted themselves, and the hospitals were cleaned up. However, even down to the beginning of this century they provided little more than custodial care. A patient was given a bed, a bath, and some food, such basic attention and little more. Hospital staffs did not have our knowledge of medicine, our drugs, or our surgical procedures, and they just did the best they could.

Many of the early hospitals in the United States were related to churches, and the first Baptist hospital was started in 1890 in St. Louis by a Baptist layman. He was a physician, a gentle and kindly man, who knew of some aging women with no one to care for them. He tried to get them into city and county hospitals, but could not, so he rented an old residence and started a hospital with less than a dozen beds. The people of his church and the Baptists of the area learned about his work, and they took over its administration and its maintenance. This was the quiet beginning of a great tradition and today Baptist hospitals are scattered over the country.

I don't think there is any point in my insisting on what everybody already knows: that the "hospital" quality of these Baptist hospitals is of the highest. Of course they are good hospitals or they could not continue. No medical institution can sustain itself today on a record of good intentions, no matter how sincere or devout; and a Baptist hospital must meet the strictest standards of the Joint Commission of Accreditation of Hospitals. We can, therefore, accept without question the equipment, staff, and experience of Baptist hospitals and be certain of their scientific ability to care for the sick.

But is a Baptist hospital just another place to go for an illness or an operation? Are the latest medical practices, the most carefully trained staff, and the greatest hospital efficiency the total meaning of such a hospital? I don't believe so. To me, a Baptist hospital is a good deal more than all its medicine and surgery. It stands squarely in the middle ground between Science and Religion, and I believe that along with its scientific credentials, its license to operate under the state laws, and its hospital accreditation, it must also have Christian credentials, intangible perhaps, but unmistakable.

A person in any hospital asks himself so many questions. The first usually is: "Why am I here? What have I done to deserve this?" Often the answer is: "I can't remember what I am guilty of, but I wouldn't be this sick if God weren't punishing me for something."

We in a Baptist hospital don't think about sickness in this way. Sickness need not mean punishment. It can be a treasured experience. Here is what I mean: For so long we may have heard of friends or relatives getting sick, being hurt or disabled, even dying; but this has never been personal to us. These things happen to other people.

Then we ourselves become ill, and there are some truly meaningful hours in illness. One is when a man discovers his own mortality and finds out that he is not a permanent fixture on earth, that he is going to die. He is not built for permanence and there is nothing about him that does not wear out. If this realization comes in a Christian hospital, with Christian men and women near at hand, with Christian resources to help him understand the discovery, then the man is way ahead.

Take, for example, the visit of the hospital minister on the day, or even the night, before surgery. Most people facing surgery are less concerned about the operation itself than about whether or not they will wake up. The hospital minister can never give assurance that he cannot back up, but he can discuss simply and quietly what resources and facilities are available to care for the patient and help him recover. Sometimes a person coming to surgery for the first time does not know oxygen is supplied to him, in the pipeline here, and that there are people who will never take their eyes off him while he is being operated on, who will watch his blood pressure and his heart beat anticipating any need that he may have. He is not just lying there uncared for on a table with a surgeon operating and a nurse standing by. There is a whole span of service to care for him. This is reassurance; this is support; and along with it, if the patient wishes, there can be the spiritual assurance that so many of us want to hear when it is spoken by a Christian man such as the hospital minister.

In the visit of this hospital minister there is a great responsibility, and there must be caution. We are a Baptist hospital, but we respect, in every sense, the variety of religious backgrounds of the people who come to us. We give the respect to them and to their religion that we expect to receive. We do not attempt to impose on people, and above all else we consistently refuse to look on the bedridden person as a candidate for quick conversion. We are always willing to knock, but the patient must open the door.

Another blessing that comes to us in disease or in the sharp test of surgery is the experience of accepting without question the remedy that is proposed for us. This may be the first time that we have ever put ourselves completely in the hands of someone else. For the first time we say: "I am dependent on these people and I am helpless without them. I must trust my nurse when she brings me something to take. I must trust my doctor that this drug, which he has chosen for me, will help me." Or a man will believe what he has heard his examining surgeon say, accepting without question the decision that the diseased tissues must be removed in order to protect the rest of the body. It is a wonderful experience to be dependent on someone else and put your total faith in him. For this to happen in Christian surroundings sometimes leads to a greater trust and faith in One Who is more than human.

The third blessing in the experience of illness comes when the patient accepts the consequences of his illness. He may have a coronary and this says to him that he is sick, but there may be no immediate danger. His problem, therefore, is his acceptance of illness and its consequences. What will it mean to his vocation? Will he have to change jobs? If he has been doing physical labor he may now be disqualified. Or maybe he has had an amputation. He walks into the hospital with two feet and is limping out with one. What will this do to him? What will it mean?

What happens to a man is never so important as what, with God's help, he makes of it. This is the teaching of the Christian Gospel, and this is the Gospel that is taught, whether spoken or not, in a Christian hospital. It can mean more to a man who is ill or disabled than the care of the doctors or even the surgeon's restorative skill.

But while the staff may be friendly in a Baptist hospital, and truly concerned with the spiritual and physical needs of its patients, the hospital itself is like all others in that it must pay its way and maintain itself as a business undertaking. In the early days, when only custodial care was provided, the matter of finances was no great problem. There was comparatively little cost in such care, and since most of the cases were charity cases anyhow the churches simply paid for them. Nowadays financing a hospital is a multimillion dollar yearly proposition, and such financing is particularly difficult in a Baptist hospital because each probably starts out with a considerable debt. Such hospitals prefer to borrow the money, and pay interest on it, to build their hospitals rather than to accept money offered them by the national government through the Hill-Burton Act. Baptists, by and large, will take none of this proffered assistance because they refuse to look on the national government as a source of financial aid. This is a part of the old Baptist teaching, infinitely wise and enduringly stubborn, that the church and the state are separate and for the good of both they must continue to be so.

No matter how big the debt, it is our belief that a hospital should be on the side of the sick person and we hold our charges as low as possible, doing our best to keep a drag on the trend of rising hospital expenses. This is not easy when one considers, for instance, that an open-heart operation often requires that eighteen persons shall be on duty and it calls for the use of very complicated equipment. The cost of such an operation is between four and five thousand dollars. We have seldom had a patient who could pay for it. We have never yet turned such a patient away.

A Baptist hospital makes its full resources available to people, even those least able to pay; but there are various ways in which a charity service can be rendered, and we feel that the right way is very important. With us it must always be done in such a manner as to preserve dignity and worth, and this means that while we will see to it that a patient's needs are cared for, he must do his part also. We have a firm belief that handouts undermine a person's self respect. This is our argument with the welfare state and we are unvarying and unyielding about it. A patient of ours must pay something. It may be no more than five dollars for a five-hundred-dollar expense. If he hasn't five dollars, perhaps he has one dollar. If he hasn't one dollar, let him come to us with a quarter and we will accept it.

This respect for the individual is bound up in our belief that the Christian church and its related institutions must always be concerned with a person's dignity. We try to be especially careful about this *inside* the hospital, making sure that no person with us is ever known as a charity case. As a matter of fact, there is no record of charity beyond the administrator's office, and it is never spoken of by anyone unless the person himself discusses it. What a patient gets is determined by his medical needs. If a physician feels that one of his patients needs a private room for medical reasons and there is only one private room available, even though it is the most expensive room in the building, he gets it. The patient is Mr. Somebody, Miss Somebody, or Mrs. Somebody. He is always a person of importance to us, as well as to himself, and is never simply a charity case.

The costs must be met, however, and a hospital's income for charity service is generally dependent on two main sources. People, out of gratitude for their own good health and feeling that they would like to share in restoring the health of someone else, sometimes send contributions. Then there are those whom we have cared for in former years and whose circumstances have changed; these people remember. Sometimes a hundred dollars or fifty dollars or one dollar will come out of a clear sky with no name to let us know the donor. There has been enough of this to convince me that many people live by the wonderful old adage that "a man is blessed who gives and forgets and who receives and remembers." There are individuals, too, who leave bequests in their wills, and the churches sometimes take a special offering for a hospital. The Southern Baptist Convention allots a small amount of money to its hospitals. But all of it together does not usually meet the bills and we have to go back to the unending job of finding resources to meet the needs.

I mentioned respect for each person, and we find in our hospitals that this Baptist insistence on the dignity of an individual, whether a charity case or a well-known benefactor of the hospital, has a great meaning for young doctors. Some of those who come to us may have studied in large medical schools and taken their internship in affiliated hospitals. The sheer mass of work in such surroundings may have tended to focus all their attention on diseased organs or distressed functions only. They may have come out well educated and with a lot of experience but without once having encountered the concept of the patient as a person.

This concept is so fundamental with us, both in our hospital practice and in our church belief, that almost inevitably the young doctor who comes to a Baptist hospital sees and understands the new emphasis. I have found that these doctors, no matter how scientifically cold they may have imagined themselves to be, learn to like the idea of dealing with people as human beings. Then, too, this kind of dealing brings them closer to the older physicians on our staff, who have long looked on patients as individual men and women. Beyond a diseased gall bladder or ruptured appendix, patients may need some understanding and friendly consideration, as well as medicines and operations. This point of view in the older men is seen and gradually accepted by the younger men, and I have had them tell me that it adds to their enjoyment of their practice.

While I am writing about doctors I would like to say that I have come to believe that the members of the medical profession, whether young or old, are much maligned. One hears of their money grubbing and their efforts to benefit themselves, but I have never seen those on the staffs of our hospitals demonstrate this in any way. We have yet to be refused by any physician when asked to give his service or skill, even though there was no chance whatever of compensation. In these hospitals the staff give of themselves day after day, year after year, and there is no grudging about it either; instead, there is a kind of joy in their giving. They are wonderful people, these doctors. I am closely associated with them every day and I ought to know something about them, and I believe that their response to charity should be known.

Besides the doctors, there are a lot of other people in hospitals who deserve praise. I am a Baptist preacher really, not a hospital administrator, and so I can look on hospital people in a slightly different way than if all my training had been strictly scientific or administrative. I know that the people who work in hospitals are not just ordinary people, because I have seen them, in their work and in their service, live in the midst of sickness and pain, and I have seen them dedicated to the sole purpose of ending sickness and easing pain.

I think sometimes that the glamour goes too much to the professional people: the nurse and the doctor. They deserve every bit of praise and all the honor that anyone can give them, but there are some other people in a hospital who should not be overlooked. We had a letter from a former patient not long ago who was very conscious, so she said, of the hands that were at her service while she was in the hospital. "They were strong hands," she said, "yet gentle; they were probing but kind." She wrote on in this vein until I began to wonder why we let people come and go without knowing more about a hospital, about *all* the people who take care of them. I wished that this woman could have seen some of the other hands that are here. Some may be gnarled, but they control machinery more delicate than a watch. Some are calloused, and may be very worn as they push the mops to keep the place clean. There are all kinds of hands in a hospital, and some, one can say, are just as essential as the gentle hands of a nurse or the strong, skilled hands of a surgeon. A hospital is a strange world, in a way, for beyond the nurse's cap and the doctor's stethoscope is another world of people, all working to care for the sick. I know it to be a goodly world of kind and gentle people.

A Baptist hospital is established, of course, to care for the physical needs of men and women and to provide compassion; but we should all understand that it is here primarily because of the nature of God and the example of Jesus. The teaching of the Gospel is that God is concerned with whatever happens to people; Jesus himself showed this concern and sympathy whenever he encountered human need. The care of the sick is a part of the Christian mission, a part of evangelism; and we will therefore go on opening hospitals and caring for the sick. We will also see that these hospitals are more than merely places of medicine and surgery; we will do our best to maintain them as Christian institutions where a man can find an answer to his spiritual longings as well as his physical needs.

# They Look After You When Age Comes

Gerald I. Gingrich
Division of Institutional Ministries
American Baptist Convention

Never has there been more abundant evidence of the truth in the saying, "Don't underestimate the power of a woman," than in the story of the beginning of our Ministries of Mercy. Women were responsible for the first Baptist home for the aged in this country.

It all began shortly after the Civil War. Thousands of men, many of them married, had been killed. Thousands of others were heading into the West that had been newly opened and was beckoning with gold and free land. The men were taking their wives and children but were leaving behind the older people to join the widows of the soldiers. This was long before any insurance plans and pension protection, long before Social Security, and many of the elderly people were destitute.

So, in the midst of this loneliness and need, we encounter the Baptist women and see evidence of their power. Recognizing the plight of the older people, the women went about passing the word: "Tell the ladies whom you meet to think about a home for the aged!" They thought and they planned and they held a great street fair on lower Broadway. With the money they raised, they established in New York the first Baptist home for the aged in the United States. This was in 1869, and that home is still operating, now located on Henry Hudson Parkway and serving over two hundred residents, one of our finest retirement homes.

At one time many churches and denominational leaders believed it was no job of the church to care for the aged. This, they said, was the responsibility of the community and the government. The church was concerned with evangelism, the winning of individuals to personal commitment to Jesus Christ. Later, however, this thinking changed, and there began an evangelism of the total person in all stages of his life. These changes have played their part, of course, in the establishment of Baptist homes for the aged.

The early homes were charitable and often dominated by a patronizing attitude toward the people they took in. Later, after they ceased to be entirely charitable, they adopted a plan by which an applicant was required to turn over everything he had, to sign away his every asset to the home, and the home in return promised to house and feed and care for him for the rest of his life.

All that is different now. For one thing our newer homes could not operate on this plan; it would not be financially feasible to do so. Another reason for the change was the psychological effect on people who surrendered their financial independence. One of the most crippling of all fears is the fear of domination, and once a person has signed away his financial assets he has handed to another at least a part of the control of himself.

In changing the ways of operation, new plans of all kinds had to be made and the program for Baptist retirement homes was not only revised but practically made over. Today one such retirement home can be an apartment-type for people completely able to care for themselves physically. Another is a group-apartment, where personal care can be given by a matron, house mother, or administrator. A third is a home where the residents need constant infirmary attention. The ideal, perhaps, is a combination of all these types in one building so that an elderly person can move in and know that whatever his situation or condition in the future he can live on at this one facility.

Each Baptist home is autonomous and the staff makes its own decisions, but the majority have a rule that a resident must be over sixty-five and must be ambulatory at the time of admittance. Some homes will take patients already bedridden, and most will accept residents who have some chronic health problem; but the usual requirement is the one of age and that a person be ambulatory and able to take care of himself.

In regard to money the custom is that an applicant pays a "founder's fee" or "entrance gift." Depending on the home he enters, the fee can be very little at one but rise into thousands at another. At one of the newest and most elaborate, Orangewood in Phoenix, Arizona, the range is from $4,000 to $13,700, the amount being determined by the kind of accommodation the person specifies.

He can get a Studio for one person—living room, bed alcove, bath, patio, lounge, and kitchen in common with ten other units—for an entrance fee of $4,000 and a monthly charge of $102. From this type of accommodation the apartments rise in cost and comfort until a man and woman, taking one of the larger apartments at Orangewood, can get a living room, dining space, kitchen, two bedrooms, two baths, patio—a total of 945 square feet—for an entrance fee of $13,700 and $242 a month.

Monthly charges cover maintenance, utilities, daily noon meal, medical insurance and care, and any special care that may have been agreed on by the resident and the home.

Such payments as these are a good deal too high for many people, but there are other homes with entrance fees of $2,500, $1,000, $300, where the difference between payment and cost is made up by the local churches. These homes are never charitable institutions and an entrance fee of some kind, regardless of its amount, is always paid either by the applicant, by his family, by a service club, anonymously and privately, or perhaps by the Deacons' Fund of some church. Dignity and self-respect are always maintained.

It is possible, though, that the time may come when the resident cannot meet his monthly charges. What then? By this time he is probably eligible for old-age assistance by the state, and in many cases this will cover the account. If not, there are churches or clubs or individuals who will see to the care of an old person in one of our homes. I know of none ever having been turned out, and I cannot conceive of it.

In case a resident becomes infirm and bedridden in a home where there is an infirmary on the property, he is moved there and stays as long as the doctor thinks he should. If he must be hospitalized for surgery the home will bear the cost, unless the resident himself is carrying a medical insurance plan. If it becomes necessary for him to go to the state hospital he would follow the regular admission policy of any other resident of the state.

What about life in these homes, the ways and the customs? How do the people live? What do they do?

This is difficult to say because each home has its own ways and customs, and there can be no standard answer. The desire is always to preserve as many of the freedoms of the individual as possible, recognizing that each of them has *his* ways, and to keep any rules carefully within reason and to the minimum. The residents are as free in every way and as independent as residents in any community.

In the program of meals at Phoenix, for example, anybody is free to take breakfast or supper in his room or to take it with a group. The one meal that is obligatory is the noon meal. We have found this is necessary to control diet. Older people, if left to their own devices, may not be careful about balanced diets. But even the noon meal is served from 11:30 to 1:00, and a resident can come at any time, sit at any table as in a restaurant, either with friends or alone, if a table is vacant. The menu is printed the day before and posted on the bulletin board, and he can have been thinking about what he is going to choose to eat.

There is always an attempt to meet not only the needs of the individual but also his desires. He is free to come and go as he pleases—free to go to church, to the movies, to visit his relatives, or have them visit him. The idea is to keep him living as normal a life as possible, and a valuable part of this plan is for him to continue his activities in the outside community. We hope that he will stay active in his church, keep up his membership in Kiwanis or the Lions, and participate in the Golden Age Club. If he once sold insurance, let him go on selling insurance—at an easier pace perhaps. If a woman has retired from full-time teaching, let her stay active as a supply teacher.

There are religious services at the home and everyone is invited, but no one is required to come to them. Many of the homes have no limiting factor on admittance, either in regard to race or religion, and a non-Baptist can be admitted in exactly the same way as some Baptist deacon or even a minister. Other homes have both a church and a residence requirement; an applicant must have been a member of a Baptist church for some specified number of years and that church must be within the area of a particular Association. Yet even in these restricted homes, once a person is a resident his personal life is completely his own and he can attend services or not just as he pleases. Some of the homes have chaplains, but they do not visit except where they are invited. It is hoped that the people will attend prayer meeting or any special services in the home; it is hoped even more that they will continue their membership in their own church and go on worshiping and working in it.

There are not only religious services at all the homes but a wide variety of entertainment and cultural offerings. We like to be located near a university, if possible, so that the residents can share in its activities—attending concerts, hearing visiting lecturers, occasionally enrolling in classes as students, and forming study clubs of their own with university professors as teachers. A university is not the only source of study and entertainment; the Golden Age Clubs of a community also provide an incentive to study and offer programs of all kinds. Then, too, touring singers and concert artists sometimes visit the home, and magicians love to come. The residents themselves have talent shows and surprise each other with their abilities. At some homes there is space enough for gardens, and many a resident shares his vegetables with his friends and adorns their tables with his flowers. This kind of thing can lead to romance —and there has been more than one marriage in the homes.

One thing more. In most of the homes a person can have a small pet, particularly one that has long been with him. One applicant had kept a goldfish and when he met with the interviewing committee he said: "I have a goldfish; it is a large goldfish, and he has lived with me for twelve years. I cannot part with that goldfish, so you will have to let me bring him." The committee said very well, in our garden we have a small fish pond and this pond can be his home. So the man brought the fish with him and it lived there in the pond for three years. But it got into the habit in the middle of the night of jumping out of the pond and all the residents talked about erecting a fence to stop it. They didn't get around to it, and one morning they came out and there was the fish dead on the patio surrounding the pool. The residents were so fond of the fish by this time that they had him stuffed and mounted and they put him on the wall of the main dining room of the home. That will be one of the first places they will take you when you visit the home.

The "Case of the Gadabout Goldfish" is the only one I can think of in which a resident in one of our homes was so determined to get away. However, if anyone does want to leave, he certainly need not stay. There is always a trial period—thirty days, six months, three years—and if a resident leaves during this time a part of his entrance fee is returned to him. This rarely happens because we have found unofficially that people tend to live about five years longer when they come into one of our homes; they find that life is so much more meaningful and happy than on the outside.

Occasionally though a person turns out to be impossibly difficult, affecting the entire community's happiness, and when this occurs the home has the right to ask him to leave. This, too, rarely happens, because there are various and sundry ways to cope with somebody who is cranky. At many of the homes the residents meet regularly to talk about problems that concern them, to make sure that they are being well taken care of, and to plan social events and projects that interest them. They have found that a person who just refuses to co-operate can be invited into such meetings and his ways discussed openly in his presence, the other residents telling him what they feel is wrong with him and how he can change his ways to get along better in the community. This plan, with everything laid on the table by the residents themselves, is usually far better than any step the administrator might take.

The administrator has his responsibilities, however, and they are many. There was a time when he needed little more than sincerity and dedication, possibly with no formal training. Increasingly, though, he must have training in addition to his good qualities, and we have arranged a course of study for anyone considering this position.

After graduation from college or a university the man or woman will enter a seminary for one year of theological study. The second year he will enter a university school of social work, and study there for two years. He will then return to the seminary for a year's additional theological study, after which he will receive both the Master of Social Work and his Bachelor of Divinity degrees. This is the type of training that we want, and in time probably will require, in the administrators of our Baptist homes.

Such training is not too much when one considers the administrator's responsibility. The home is related to the church, and this means, for the administrator and for each person associated with him, that he is here to be of service, that he has no personal motives or thoughts of profit. People trust us because we are church-related, and they look to us for a clear and reassuring stand on religion. Religion takes on an increasing importance to aging people, even those who have had no interest in it before, and the administrator who works with them must understand this and must himself have a surety about religion and an unmistakable faith. He must also have an abiding personal interest in each person, realizing that the individual is the center of the home which is there for his welfare. These qualities—along with an ability to maintain the home, transact its business, and supervise its program centered on the individual—require a man not only of goodness but of highest professional training. This is why we believe that the dual program of study, the years of training in social work with its religious underpinning, should develop the kind of administrators we want in our Baptist homes.

Almost eighteen million Americans over sixty-five live in our country. This is a major segment of our population, and we are all becoming aware of these people among us and that they have special needs. The average age span in 1900 was forty-seven years; today it is over seventy. The government is taking this into account with its amazing development of health and welfare activities, and there is a whole new philosophy concerning the aged. They are now to be reckoned with economically, socially, politically. Never before in the history of mankind have so many people lived so many years. Never before have churches had such an opportunity for expanding their ministry for older people.

Our churches anticipate this privilege and welcome the prospect of serving these people through "homes that care."

# TELL ME
# WHAT THEY SAY

# *I Go to Church on Sunday*

Raymond L. Guffin, Jr.
Graduate Art Student
University of Georgia
Athens, Georgia

Last Sunday morning I was awakened by the sunlight shining through my bedroom windows. A cool autumn breeze rippled through the curtains and I pulled the cover over my head. My wife of three months and I, both university students with loaded schedules, had looked forward to this weekend. Here was our only time for recreation and relaxation. I lay still so as not to disturb my sleeping wife.

The chill in the air and the quietness of the Sunday morning reminded me of an experience in Marine Corps boot camp only a few autumns ago. There, a gruff old sergeant would invariably wake our platoon early on Sunday morning and march us to an amphitheater one-half mile away for a simple worship service. He would always mutter something before we started about how this was the kind of discipline from which good Marines were made. Of course, most of us construed the word "discipline" to mean punishment, and participated unenthusiastically. But, secretly, I felt refreshed after each worship service. And I think my buddies did also, though it would not have been masculine to admit it. I doubt if I could recall anything the chaplain said, but I think it was the only time during the week when I would take a moment to look myself squarely in the face for a period of personal evaluation. And I began to feel that this was vital to the growth of my character.

On this particular Sabbath morning, however, the choice of church attendance would be personal and require greater effort. I questioned my responsibility. There was no pressure, no parents to remind me, no drill sergeant to order me. I was certain that I would do God no great favor by my effort. And yet I felt a hunger for my thoughts and spirit to be raised above the routine. My wife and I were soon dressed and on our way to church.

The towering Corinthian columns caught my eye as we arrived. Why should a pagan temple design be adapted for a Christian house of worship? And why not? The original design had represented man's worship, his reach toward something greater than he. Using my practiced art student's eye, I looked at the massive simplicity of the church and I believed I knew why the old temple design had been used again for a place of worship, for there was something universally uplifting about its strength and beauty. Yet there was the greatest difference between the old and new. The original was built as an offering to some deity out of fear. This house, the one I was coming to, was built to a loving God. I was glad that I had a religion built on love. I had no fear in this house. I felt a gentleness, a sense of belonging here. We entered the sanctuary in silence.

I recognized the well-built young man going in just ahead of us as a fullback on last year's freshmen football team. I had a sudden curiosity about his presence here. Was it because of habit—or a hunger? I then asked the same question of myself. Why had I come to church today?

A silver-haired usher led us to a pew in the middle section. As I sat there my body relaxed from the rush to get to church on time. And my mind lapsed into trivial thoughts. I participated in the common ritual of watching the Sunday morning dress parade during the organ prelude. I overheard portions of hushed conversation between two teenaged girls immediately behind me. The black-robed choir members filed in, and introductory notes to the Doxology called me to attention. I suddenly had a feeling of unity with the congregation, as we joined the choir in singing.

The morning prayer by the minister was a quiet petition. Now and then I heard a phrase of the prayer, but I also found myself replaying parts of Saturday's football game. The same young football player who had entered the church just before me had scored almost at the end of the game, and I was reliving all the excitement. I remembered, though, where I was and humbly uttered a short prayer as the minister brought his to a close.

I was fully brought to the present by the morning hymn. It was a moving hymn of consecration and one that I like:

*Dear Lord and Father of Mankind,*
*Forgive our foolish ways.*
*Reclothe us in our rightful mind,*
*In purer lives Thy service find,*
*In deeper reverence, praise.*

During the announcements I let my gaze wander over the church. Always the light through the blue and the amber of the stained-glass windows had made me long to paint just that color, especially the delicate nuances of blue, but I had never been able to get it exactly. The flowers on the communion table this morning were yellow, and someone had used sprays of pine as greenery for the arrangement. I thought of something one of my art professors had said. Has anyone *ever* painted a pine tree? Thousands have tried, yes, but has anyone ever really painted a pine tree? I wished that I could and I wanted to try.

The morning anthem was appealing to me and I listened, hearing the beauty of the music, seeing the choir members, eyes lowered, a picture etched in black and white, changing rhythmically as in unison the music pages were turned. When the anthem was over and the choir sat down I eased back against my pew. Somehow I had a feeling of joy. Perhaps music sometimes surpasses words in reaching the soul. Is joy at the sound or sight of beauty a groping toward worship, a reaching toward God? I don't know, but I have felt that it may be.

The minister rose to address the congregation. He was dressed in a dark business suit, a man of medium height, older than I but not old enough to be my dad. He was more experienced than I, for he had lived longer and no doubt his experience had been different from mine. He could teach me much. But in our Baptist faith we were equal in our access to God. He was there to share a message, not hand down one. He was there to share his belief, not dictate mine.

The minister's message was the message of a prophet. And yet it was quiet and full of reason. He had translated the words of the biblical prophet into twentieth-century American. I began to feel closer to the mainstream of Christianity. I knew that my personal responsibility to God went far beyond mere church attendance. It could be met only by fulfilling my responsibilities to myself and my fellow men. I had known this when I came to church, but my coming had strengthened the knowledge and the sermon gave me a new sense of personal duty.

The minister finished his sermon, and, still speaking softly, he opened the doors of the church and gave the invitation. The choir sang a hymn reaffirming the invitation of Christ for all men to come unto Him.

As we sang, I looked toward the baptistry and remembered when I had been baptized. What did it mean to me then? What does it mean to me now? I can't say for sure, but I am glad that I did it. There is a satisfaction and a surety in it, and somehow a greater nearness to God and a closeness to Jesus. A student I had never seen before joined the church that morning and I wanted to go down and shake hands with him, and I did.

As my wife and I walked up the aisle we spoke to our friends. In the vestibule I saw one of my art professors and he spoke to me first. He was the one who had told me that no one had ever painted a pine tree.

Why had I come to church this morning in the first place? All the good that came from this particular service did not come to me every Sunday. Some Sundays the anthem was not especially beautiful; the minister did not always get his message over to me. Then why do I go to church on Sunday?

Perhaps the feeling that I call hunger to have my thoughts and spirit raised above the routine is in reality something more than that. Perhaps it is my desire to acknowledge my belief and to share in the belief of my fellow churchmen. Maybe it is to magnify my attitude of reverence, of adoration, and my gratitude to God who loves me and all mankind so much that He was willing to send his Son to teach us His way, and to let that Son suffer even death so that I and all who believe in Him might be saved. Whatever the feeling, whatever the desire or reason, it is there each Sunday morning and going to church adds to the day a sense of peace and well being.

# *Hear the Baptists Singing*

Walter Hines Sims
Secretary of Church Music Department
The Sunday School Board
Southern Baptist Convention

Singing and music have been here on earth as long as we have, for it is the nature of man to sing. It is in his heart to sing his love. It is in his soul to sing to his God. Music is a part of his worship, and when he is at church he helps make a singing congregation a worshiping congregation.

This significance of music is plain to all of us today, but it may surprise some people to learn that it took the Baptists a long time to realize it and to agree on it. Today among Baptist churches music is the fastest growing activity in all the work of the denomination, but singing at one time was not only disapproved of by the Baptists but they had an actual ban on it. Even a few decades ago music was in a pitiful plight in Baptist churches. The long story, stretching back for centuries, is a curious one, sometimes almost incredible to us now.

In the beginning, some three centuries ago in England, there was frightful contention about music in Baptist churches, and many of them would have none of it. Worship, they said, should come only from the Holy Spirit, entirely spontaneous as the Spirit moved a man, and the singing of hymns of "human composure" was evil. However, some Baptists wanted to sing, and they did, usually metrical versions of the Psalms.

Then in 1673 a Baptist pastor introduced hymn singing in his church. Here was something really to thunder against! The singing of hymns was openly directed and could not possibly be spontaneously inspired by the Holy Spirit. Such singing was "carnal formality!" (One church, split between singers and anti-singers, came up with the solution of singing one hymn each Sunday, *but at the end of the service,* thus giving the anti-singers time to get away.) The controversy was brought over to the Colonies and continued here until most Baptist churches put an end to it and got on with their singing.

They just sang, though, for there were few trained persons to direct music. Some Baptists, early in this century, began asking for improvements. Public schools were making great strides in the area of music, community singing was popular, and the new radio was exciting everybody by bringing music into the home. Spokesmen in the Southern Baptist Convention said that people heard good music for six days a week and they should not have to put up with second-rate music on Sunday.

Nothing was done, however, until 1938, when a survey was taken and revealed that in Southern Baptist churches only one choir director in five had *any* musical training—and for purposes of the survey a two-week's trip to a vacation singing school was counted as training! Several years later the Convention recommended that colleges, universities, and seminaries establish Departments of Church Music and begin the training of Ministers of Music on whom the improvement of church music so largely depends. These men are truly ministers, and often are ordained by their congregation *for the specific purpose of ministering through music.* They do not baptize or perform weddings, but, along with their ministering through musical responsibilities, they take full part in the church programs and at all times are aids to the pastor. They are the "under-shepherds" of the church.

A Minister of Music must be a good musician and well trained in voice, instrument, and other areas of music. In preparing for this ministry a young man or woman—for women, too, can be Ministers of Music—will first be graduated from some recognized university or college, taking the B.M. or A.B. degree (usually in music) or the B.S. degree (usually with a major in music). They then enter a seminary for advanced training, and there the Bachelor of Church Music can be taken in one year, the Master of Church Music in two years. The Doctor of Church Music calls for three years or more of study.

Hundreds of churches today need dedicated and talented Ministers of Music and are earnestly asking for them. The requests cannot be satisfied because not enough young people have heard the call in music and prepared themselves to answer it.

A Minister of Music coming to a church must always observe one great precaution: he must make certain that he does not try to start at *his* level of music. He must start *where the people are.* His purpose, though, is that they do not just stay there.

Almost surely he will begin a program of "graded choirs," developing choirs for Beginners, Primaries, Juniors, Intermediates, Young People, and Adults. He will correlate this music with the Sunday School lessons and the Training Union lessons. If a child goes to a choir rehearsal for his particular age group on Wednesday afternoon, an alert Minister of Music will make certain that the people in charge of that group will have some songs that fit in with next Sunday's lesson. Graded choirs range from earliest childhood through adulthood, with choirs and small ensembles for men and women.

In our Southern Baptist churches we have hundreds of Junior choirs, ages nine through twelve. One year we wanted something special for them, so we conceived of a little cantata written in their language. It was called "Lo! A Star." It tells simply about the night that Jesus was born, the shining of the star, and the coming of the shepherds. It is a beautiful musical narrative of some fifteen or twenty minutes. One of the Junior choirs recorded it for distribution along with the music, and now the children in many churches sing it at Christmas time.

At present we are working on an oratorio, "Behold the Glory of the Lamb," which will be presented at one of our nationwide conferences. Later it will be used in the churches by choirs that are trained to sing it.

This talk about cantatas and oratorios must never let us lose sight of the fine hymn singing under the high wooden steeples of village churches, or the all-day singing at some crossroad church where dinner is served on the ground. This is the music that these people know; this is their worship; and it rises sweet and clear to the throne of God. Since it is heard in heaven we will honor it here on earth. There can never be any belittlement of music that is sung in worship.

Paul, in Colossians 3:16, cites music of the church as having three forms: Psalms and hymns and spiritual songs. The Psalms usually are couched in the higher forms of choral music. Hymns and Gospel songs are music of the people, congregational music. I like to think of the hymn as music which characterizes great and solemn praise, man singing his adoration to God. The hymn is marked by dignity and objectivity; often it is majestic; and usually it has stood the long test of time, some of the hymns having been sung for centuries. "Holy, Holy, Holy, Lord God Almighty" is unmistakably a hymn—solemn, majestic, enduring.

The Gospel song, while less solemn and profound, should never be put in unfortunate contrast with the hymn because these songs too are worshipful in spirit and intent. They are the people directly singing their praise and bearing witness. Such Gospel songs as "I will sing the wondrous story of the Christ Who died for me" and "Blessed assurance, Jesus is mine! Oh, what a foretaste of glory divine" tell of what Christ did for a poor unworthy sinner and of the assurance that wells up in his heart when Christ becomes his Savior.

In the Gospel song there is almost always the intimacy and personal experience that one finds in folk music, the lonely man on the prairie singing *his* story to the stars, the worshiping man revealing *his* salvation experience in "the Christ Who died for me." In the Gospel song often there is also something of the white or Negro spiritual, the purest of all folk music welling up in the yearning of a man or a people.

Adoration in hymns and the evangelistic concept in Gospel songs are well known, but not so well known is another distinction of both hymn and song. They both are used for the teaching of doctrines. There was a time in England, and also later in the Colonies, when there was a shortage of hymnals and also few people who could read. It was not uncommon that the hymns were "lined out" to the people, a deacon or the pastor himself reading a line and the people singing it. After a while somebody had the idea that these people who could not read could be taught the Baptist doctrines by lining them out. Moreover, such teaching would be remembered and hummed the next day as the man walked the street or sung as he worked in his field or shop. This kind of teaching flourished and became an effective means of conveying our doctrine and scriptural truth to the believer. For example, the first American Baptist hymnal, *Hymns and Spiritual Songs*, contained 138 hymns, of which 16 were on baptism, 74 on the Lord's Supper, and the remaining 48 were spiritual songs.

Doctrine still plays its part in church music. No matter how fine the hymn or sweet the song, a question today is always asked before we publish it: Is it true according to the scriptures and sound according to Baptist doctrine? There is a great common body of hymnody throughout Protestant churches and many of the hymns are sung by all denominations; "O God, Our Help in Ages Past" and "O Worship the King" are good examples of hymns that everyone sings. It is when a hymn contains a doctrinal teaching that it is examined most closely and may be rejected by the editors of the hymnal.

I will show you what I mean. There is a hymn in our Baptist hymnal called "Our Best," Number 437, that begins: "Hear ye the Master's call, 'Give Me thy best'!" But in our Baptist hymnal that hymn has only two stanzas. The third stanza is omitted. It says: "Night soon comes on apace, day hastens by, Workman and work must face testing on high. Oh, may we in that day find rest, sweet rest, which God has promised those who do their best." But that is not Baptist doctrine. Baptists believe that salvation is only by grace and the acceptance of the Lord Jesus Christ as a personal Savior. It is not a matter of doing our best. A man, no matter how good he is, must have Jesus Christ as his Savior. So the editors of the Baptist hymnal left out the third stanza because it is not true Baptist doctrine.

This concern with doctrine brings up an obvious question: Are there any strictly *Baptist* hymns? The answer is no. Some of the great hymns of the world were written by the Baptists: "Come, Thou Fount of Every Blessing," "Blest Be the Tie that Binds;" and Samuel F. Smith, a Baptist preacher in Massachusetts, wrote a hymn in 1832 that was first sung on July the fourth of that year: "My Country, 'Tis of Thee." Such hymns belong to everyone, and there are any number of these inter-denominational or non-denominational hymns. In our Baptist hymnal, for example, there are a score of hymns by the Wesleys, the founders of Methodism; and Number 60, "Lead, Kindly Light," was written by Cardinal Newman of the Roman Catholic Church.

We would like, of course, for more Baptists to write hymns and spiritual songs, and so we sponsor a hymn-writing contest in the Southern Baptist Convention. One year the competition is in hymn writing, the next in anthems; and we are getting some very good entries. We hope when we next revise the hymnal to have a number of new hymns written by Baptists in it.

Occasionally in a discussion of church music someone will raise the question of emotionalism, especially in regard to revivals and the singing at the time of decision and conversion. It is asked if invitation hymns in such surroundings may not have an emotional effect that will influence a man beyond an ordinary decision. Of course music can make an emotional appeal and emotions play their part in a man's answer to the call of God. At the time of conversion all of a man is given to God, his mind and body, his heart and soul, his thinking and feelings, and certainly his emotions.

A man at such a meeting hears the hymn or Gospel song inviting him to accept Christ, and there wells up within him a tremendous feeling of repentance, of desire for worship, of awe, of adoration. It is a soul-cleansing experience, coming as it does after the pastor has presented the message and issued the invitation. The man is thinking of his conviction of sin, of all that he should be repenting of, of his need for a Savior and his acceptance of Christ. This is working in his heart, in his soul, and he hears: "Just as I am, without one plea, but that thy blood was shed for me." He may sit there a while longer, pondering, groping, wavering in the blending of his feelings and the music, until the moving power of the Holy Spirit is strong upon him and he stands and clearly sounds his answer: "O Lamb of God, I come! I come!"

# *My Church and My State*

Harold Stassen
President
1963–1964
American Baptist Convention

My church is Baptist. My state is the United States. I am an American Baptist.

What does this mean in terms of the separation of church and state? For one thing, it means that by tradition for centuries, and by position today, I am among the stoutest and most persistent supporters of this principle.

And what does the phrase mean? Many long articles have been written about it. Numerous speeches have been delivered on it. Multiple court decisions have been issued applying it.

It means that the government should not dominate or direct the religious worship of the people. It means that no Church organization should control or supervise the actions of the government. It is a close companion of religious liberty.

But it does not mean that the people should be separated from their relationship to both church and state. Herein arises some of the confusion, some of the uncertainty, some of the needless controversy.

The state is involved directly or indirectly in almost every part of our lives, and the church is concerned with every aspect of human existence. Thus church and state inevitably meet in their common involvement in the life of man.

The relationship of both church and state to the people is not only a fact, it is a fact which the church must accept and welcome. Biblical scholarship shows that Christ was concerned for the whole man, not just his religious beliefs; and the tragic experience of the church in early Nazi Germany has taught us all the dangers of emphasizing spiritual life with a neglect of our everyday existence.

As a Christian layman and citizen of the United States, I believe these four statements should describe the public-spiritual relationship: separation of church and state, concern of church for state, concern of state for church, subordination of both to God.

As to the first of these statements, *separation of church and state*—early in the history of the American Colonies, Baptists in small churches from Maine to South Carolina struggled courageously to practice their religion free from any authority but God's. Roger Williams fled persecution in Massachusetts because of his non-conformist views and later established the First Baptist Church of Providence, Rhode Island. Thirty-four ministers were imprisoned in the Colony of Virginia for "disturbing the peace" when they preached what they felt was the Word of God. The first President of Harvard, Henry Dunster, was summarily dismissed in 1652 by the Overseers for publicly proclaiming his Baptist views. In North Carolina Colony marriages performed by Baptist ministers were at one time held to be void. In Massachusetts Colony when Baptists refused to pay tax money to support the state church, their property was confiscated and taken from them.

While recounting these early experiences it is important to remember that Baptists did not isolate themselves from the state, as many European Anabaptists did. Baptists were among the most loyal soldiers and supporters of the American Revolution, and Baptists were one important pressure group which insisted that the First Amendment, the first item of the Bill of Rights, be part of the Constitution.

That critical First Amendment summarizes what separation of church and state meant to the eighteenth-century Baptists: "Congress shall make no law respecting an establishment of religion, . . ." *i.e.*, no state church will be encouraged; and "Congress shall make no law . . . prohibiting the free exercise thereof [religion] . . .", *i.e.*, complete freedom of individual conscience.

Separation of church and state today means essentially what it did two centuries ago. The state cannot tell the church what to preach or tell individuals what to believe; and the church, in turn, cannot ask for state money or official influence to support religious activities. Congress and the judiciary have protected the religious liberties guaranteed in the First Amendment.

It was in applying and interpreting this article of the Constitution that the Supreme Court forbade worship services which included the reading of the King James version of the Bible in the public schools; and the courts are now considering how much of parochial school education is specifically religious and how much is identical to the public education supported by tax money.

In understanding separation of church and state it is important to realize what that separation does *not* mean. There is nothing about being a Christian and a Baptist which prevents one from being a loyal citizen, and there is nothing about being a citizen which prevents one from being a Baptist. Separation of church and state does not prevent church property from being tax free, and all the armed services have chaplains paid with government money. Many churches feel there is nothing inconsistent about having an American flag on one side of the sanctuary and a Christian flag on the other, or urging their members to vote on election day. More important, many Baptists feel that our religious convictions compel us to be concerned for the state.

With the second statement, *concern of the church for the state*, let me illustrate with an example. One Sunday morning, after the benediction, a loyal member of my church came up to shake my hand. "It must be very difficult to be a Christian in politics," she said. I knew that she was a busy housewife and mother, whose source of political information was the Philadelphia newspapers, which lately have devoted many columns to charges and countercharges about corruption in government. She meant her remark as a compliment, as an expression of approval for one who is simultaneously a deacon and a politician. Instead of answering politely, "thank you," I explained that it is in fact probably equally difficult to be a Christian student or businessman or mother. Every Christian must try to guide his actions by the teachings of his religion, even though every human realizes that issues are sometimes ambiguous and decisions are sometimes wrong.

I thought about that conversation later as I drove home. It would be difficult for me, I decided, to be a Christian and *not* be a politician, or at least not be concerned about the interaction between man and government.

As Paul says: "Now there are diversities of gifts, but the same Spirit. And there are differences of administration, but the same Lord."

But another important reason why I am a politician is that my early goals and ideas were formed by a Christian family and a Baptist church, where I learned that the church should be concerned for the state. My Sunday School taught me that Christ wants us to feed the hungry, help the sick, visit those in prison, and give water to the thirsty, and to seek peace and pursue it. Today this means that Christians must still be concerned for the sick, whether they are physically ill or emotionally twisted; with the hungry, whether they are members of my church or Buddhists in Viet Nam or Catholics in Cuba; with the imprisoned, whether they are criminals behind prison bars or minority groups chained by hidden prejudices and social inequality.

Of course, this is the task of every individual Christian and every local Baptist church. I never minimize the importance of Christian individuals and church institutions working to alleviate the human suffering in the world.

But every Christian should recognize and rejoice in the fact that one way to "help the sick" is to provide free medical care for those too poor to buy it. "Feed the hungry" sometimes means retraining the unemployable or sending food to a country which needs it. One way to "visit those in prison" is to rehabilitate prisoners or pass just laws or correct unhealthy social situations. Another way is to build good schools to teach children to think freely, and to prepare them for a steady job.

Certainly governmental action in the area of social justice is no excuse for laziness in the individual Christian. But we must always remember that devout Christians are still people. Without policemen someone would give in to the temptation to steal; without social security someone would ignore the need of his neighbor. We must also remember that one Christian, or even a large group of Christians, simply cannot handle the problems of the world. If a local policeman is unfair to a member of your church you can complain to the chief of police and, if necessary, take the case into court; but if you read in the paper that Castro is persecuting Christians in Cuba, or the Portuguese are killing Angolan leaders, you alone can do very little. Through your elected and appointed officials you can do a great deal.

With the third statement, *concern of the state for the church,* let me say that when I speak of concern of the state for the church, I do not mean, of course, that the state should help any particular church. Instead I mean that the government of the United States should recognize continually the importance of religious conviction in developing our great country. For example, the Declaration of Independence states "that all men are . . . endowed by their Creator with certain inalienable Rights," and the Northwest Ordinance provides tax-free land for a church in every community. Throughout our history national leaders have invoked the blessing of God on their actions; and citizens have prayed for the nation, the president, and those in civil authority. Religious leaders and religious beliefs have played an active part in the founding, reforming, and preserving of our country. The most recent example of this is the present agitation for racial justice. Many of the leaders are clergymen; many of the meeting places are churches; many of the songs are hymns; and, most important, the whole movement and the non-violent method are religious concerns.

Concern of the state for the church means that we as citizens must constantly remember our Christian heritage. While the civil rights of atheists must always be protected, we should never deny the importance that religion has had in our country or forget our national attitudes and policies in the light of our religious faith.

There is a special need for such a change in the field of foreign policy. The first axiom of current foreign policy stresses national self-interest. This principle on which our policy is now based seems to me to reflect a serious shortcoming.

We should instead try to make our foreign policy more consistent with the teachings of Christ, replacing narrow nationalism with Christian concern. The first consideration of our policy should not be the narrow self-interests of the United States but rather the interests of all humanity under God.

As to the last statement, *subordination of both to God*, it is all too often that the church and the state, and we as individual citizens and Christians, underestimate or forget the power of God. We must constantly remember that the laws of God are not necessarily the laws of the state, and that the wishes of God are not necessarily expressed in the church. Both church and state must act in humility rather than in arrogance. When we feel our church or our state has failed, we must also remember that God can do wonders with failure.

Baptists have traditionally fought for freedom of the individual to act as he believes God guides him. We have never accepted the authority of the state or the church as absolutely binding on man's conscience.

When Peter was questioned by the Sadducees and told not to preach in Jesus' name again, he replied, "We must obey God rather than men," angering the high council so much that they wanted to kill him. Gamaliel kept Peter and the others from harm by saying, "if this counsel or this work be of men, it will come to nought: But if it be of God, ye cannot overthrow it; lest haply ye be found even to fight against God." Peter's obedience to God rather than to the Sanhedrin and Gamaliel's wise advice are important to keep in mind as we criticize the actions of others.

Subordination of the laws of the state to the laws of God is the basis upon which the Baptist minister, Martin Luther King, Jr., established the well-known movement for non-violent insistence upon civil rights for all, as he described in his letter from the Birmingham jail. Furthermore, he stated, this is not new. It was seen in the refusal of Shadrach, Meshach, and Abednego to obey the laws of Nebuchadnezzar because a higher moral law was involved. It was practiced by the early Christians who were willing to face death or the chopping block rather than submit to certain unjust laws of the Roman Empire.

Yes, the Baptist denomination has an exceptional history. Its principles have a sharp focus today. They will have an impact tomorrow. And much of this relationship has been, is now, and will be to and through the state, although separate, as both are involved in the lives of all humanity on this earth under God.

# *On My Baptist Faith*

Brooks Hays
President
1958–1959
Southern Baptist Convention

The famous Baptist theologian and teacher Dr. Kenneth Scott Latourette of Yale University is said to have told an inquirer: "I am a Baptist by inheritance, inertia, and conviction." This is close enough to my own experience to make it a good beginning. If my father and mother had not been Baptists, and I had not been brought up in a Baptist home, I would probably have wound up in another church. Most of us are started in our church membership by our parents, and we usually keep in that path. This is the "inertia" that Dr. Latourette was talking about, the old law of physics that matter will continue in uniform motion in a straight line unless acted upon by some external force.

Sometimes we have powerful external forces acting upon us, and sometimes we may let them get us off the track that our parents set for us, but most of us usually follow our parents so far as church membership is concerned. I don't believe, though, that it is enough for a man just to follow along in the church and in the faith even of his parents. Beyond any church inheritance, and certainly beyond any inertia, he must develop his own personal convictions. This is essential to Baptists. We don't believe that a man is born with beliefs. He must develop them for himself.

Dr. Walter Rauschenbusch, a famous Baptist theologian, has a fine reference to this, and I would like to quote it: "We are Americans because we are born so," he said. "But it is our duty and our right clearly and increasingly to understand what our country stands for and to adopt as our personal principles those ideals of democracy and equality on which our national life is founded. We are Americans by birth, but we must become Americans by personal conviction. In the same way we may be Baptists by birth, but we must become Baptists by conviction. And no man is a true Baptist until his inherited tendency has been transformed into conscious purpose."

I think it is fine to point out to every boy and girl—and every man and woman, for that matter—that the surest title to the great legacy of Baptist truths is by personal acquisition rather than by heredity rights. So I started out with a fine Baptist inheritance from my parents, and I continue to this day to be pleased and proud of it; but I learned early that a man needs to develop his own convictions as he goes along. What is the use in Baptists teaching the great principle of individual liberty and religious freedom unless we as individuals use it, unless each man exercises this freedom to develop his own beliefs and convictions for himself? I stand so firmly on this great Baptist principle that I intend to go along with it forever. In this I am like my friend, Dr. S. L. Stealey, who says, "If I am separated from the Baptists they will leave me; I will never leave them."

My boyhood in Russellville, Arkansas, was lived almost completely within a small triangle. At one corner was my home, at another the public school, and at the third was the Baptist church. This was my world and it was a good one. The part that the church played was important because my life in the congregation fortified the lessons that had been taught to me by my two devout parents. In time I became a lawyer, then went into politics, and to this day I believe that the central point of my political as well as my religious faith was profoundly influenced by the instruction I received at this small church of my boyhood. There I was taught by men who may have been unschooled, and some of them almost unlettered, but they had an unquestioning and enduring faith in the everlasting truths.

There were three basic principles in the teachings of these men and in the influence of this Baptist church that have stayed with me: a sense of human dignity and of individual worth which, in theological terms, endowed me with soul sovereignty and bade me respond to the voice of conscience; a concern for all the people around me and also for those outside my orbit; an awareness of the great world with its universal values, and a recognition of an urgent need for the compassion which I identified with my faith.

Along with the learning of these principles, I was exposed to other Baptist teachings. I came to believe so completely that the individual has access to God, without any ecclesiastical intermediation whatever, that this simple concept was built into the fiber of my religious life.

The concept came so early that I could not, and cannot now, point to the processes by which I became convinced that a church does not provide my salvation by any of its ordinances or ceremonies, but rather that the church becomes my preceptor and my shelter upon my own acknowledgment (and the church's) that I have an eternal relationship with God.

Furthermore, I faithfully accepted Baptist insistence that we should not have creeds. I have sometimes been amused, however, to see Baptist ministers and even congregations vigorously oppose departure from a set of teachings—despite our firm non-creedal position! I dared not proclaim my observation of this apparent inconsistency in my youthful years, but even then I could chuckle quietly with a Presbyterian friend who put it like this: "The difference between you Baptists and us is that we have a creed that we don't live up to; and you don't have a creed, but you live down to one." Though I found this remark amusing, I was so dedicated to the historic idea of individual freedom that I knew I could always cite my loyalty to the idea, should I ever be accused of heterodoxy.

Belief in individual freedom is a glorious feature of Baptist polity, but it is an awesome one; for in it are the risks of grading down the quality of historic Christian teaching. We must remember, therefore, that some of the standards for our individuals will depend, at least in part, on the level of our Baptist teaching and teachers. The excellence of pulpit performance and the quality of Baptist schools will always have an influence on the general level of our individualism.

In regard to my interest in people, I did not get this from my church, but undoubtedly it was greatly accentuated by the church. Through the years my relationship with people has become an increasingly enthusiastic and reverent interest; and Baptist democracy being what it is, this means with *all* people, rich people and poor people, town people and rural people, white people and colored people—ah, there's the rub! Progress, though, is being made in this relationship between white people and colored people; it is being made among Southern Baptists, as well as others, because of our belief in the Baptist tradition of democracy for all men and respect for the dignity of every man.

Even when I was young I found that the emphasis upon individualism and congregation autonomy appealed to me with an almost emotional power, although I came to realize later that there was weakness as well as strength in this Baptist position. Yet, while our church governmental practices may tend to keep us on a slightly lower common level at times, rather than soaring now and then to the possible heights of individual inspiration, I, as a matter of personal preference, subscribe to our democratic church forms and practices.

Finally, I was drawn to the Baptists by their world outlook and the missionary fervor that links us to the Korean, the Burmese, the Chinese, and other Asians; the Nigerians, the Liberians and others in Africa; the Brazilians, the Peruvians, the Chileans, and others in Latin America. Here is a challenge of the whole world and to this I can respond.

I grieve at times that this appreciation of the New Testament mandate for us to go forth to all nations does not produce a spirit of cooperativeness with an avowed ecumenicity. But still I have the authority in our Baptist emphasis on liberty for my own ecumenicity. I can predict, too, that ultimately we will recognize the ties of brotherhood linking us by a common faith to the sheep not of our Baptist fold.

As I think back over what I have written in this chapter, and as I look back over my life, examining my relationship with the people who have honored me and at the same time have summoned me to their service, I can truthfully say that I am glad I started as a Baptist by inheritance—and I am deeply grateful to God that I became a Baptist, and continue as a Baptist, by my own conviction.

# *I Have Been a Baptist All My Life*

Benjamin E. Mays
President
Morehouse College

I was born, the youngest of eight children, in a family of Baptists. My mother and father and all my brothers and sisters before me were Baptists. The truth of the matter is, I was born and brought up in a Baptist community with no other denominations close around, and the Baptist church was the center of things.

My father was a farmer and we lived out in the wide-open country with no town or village nearby, even the railroad was a good way off. The church was about four miles away and my parents used to drive there in the wagon and take us with them. I don't know how old I was when they started me in Sunday School, but by the time I was eight or nine I was taking part. We had Sunday School every Sunday and preaching once a month. My parents did not always go to Sunday School, but I went. I walked or rode a mule.

One Sunday morning when I was thirteen I was sitting in the church listening to the sermon and the morning began to be different from any other. I can't tell about it or describe it, because I don't know what happened. But when the appeal came, I got up and went down front and gave the minister my hand. I cried a little and I felt lifted up and it was a new kind of feeling. I was a boy and did not understand what had happened, but there was something with me that I had never known before and I felt a little excited and happy and very safe. This was back in 1908.

That same week I was baptized, but baptism did not produce any special feeling in me. I had already had my experience, and baptism was just something that came after.

Ever since then I have been closely associated with Baptist churches. I was ordained and have been a pastor of a church. I have been a college teacher and a college dean. Now I am president of Morehouse College in Atlanta, Georgia. Often I think of all my years as a Baptist and sometimes I ask myself about the changes that I have seen take place in Baptist churches and about things as they are now.

I don't think that I can sum up these years, because no man can really tell his inner feelings; but there are some things that I, as a Baptist, can name. For instance, the freedom in a Baptist church has always meant a very great deal to me. This freedom has been abused, and sometimes still is, but for a Baptist preacher it is a good and sure feeling to have the right to say what he thinks and believes without interference from some bishop or anybody else higher up.

Freedom in their churches has a special meaning, I believe, to Negro ministers. I am quite sure that the ablest and most powerful preachers among Negroes are Baptists, and I am also sure that this sense of church freedom has something to do with it. You get able ministers in all denominations, of course, but on the whole the Negro Baptist preachers tower above the others.

There is something in the beliefs of the Baptist—freedom of conscience, the dignity and worth of every man, each man's individual right of direct access to God—that has given the Negro preacher the power that he has, the conviction and the ability to preach and to move people. A magnetism is there, drawing large crowds to him and influencing them as he preaches. From the ecclesiastical point of view he is free because there is no hierarchy to dominate him. Then—and this is most important—in his relationship with his congregation he is free; he can tell what he believes and preach his faith.

He has a good deal more freedom in his local church, I believe, than the white minister, whether that minister be Baptist or another denomination. The Negro preacher's congregation looks up to him and he does not have to be careful, in either his preaching or his ministering, about whom he might be offending, or worry about whose toes are in the way. He just stands there and tells what is in his heart, what his soul wants to say, and he tells it in the way that God prompts him.

There have been notable changes in the Baptist churches in my time. The Baptists I knew in my early years were very unworldly, far more concerned with heaven and the hereafter than with any mundane affairs. A man was getting ready to save his soul, so it didn't matter so much what went on around him, and the preacher was not concerned with improving things in this world because he was already setting out on his journey toward Jordan. Today I believe you could not find a Baptist church anywhere without interest in the happenings of its community, or a Baptist preacher without regard for the political, economic, and social aspect of the Gospel.

It is strange, though, that with all our concern for community betterment and group enlightenment the Baptists as a denomination have not given full attention to education. It may seem that I am saying this with some bias because I myself am an educator, a college president; but, actually, I am thinking as a Baptist. We Baptists simply have not put sufficient emphasis on education, either of our ministers or our laymen. This is particularly true among Negro Baptists.

In the white Baptist churches the training of ministers compares favorably, I believe, with the training in most other denominations; but this does not apply to Negro Baptist churches. We have some powerful and outstanding Negro preachers, but we also have hundreds of others who are poorly educated and are inadequately prepared. In the democracy of our Baptist churches any man can be ordained, and then, later, by displaying his emotionalism, he may be able to attract some people to him personally; but he will also drive others from his church. I am thinking particularly about young people. Any uneducated, untrained minister cannot continue to impress the young people of today, and the time may come when they will leave his church.

Baptist churches can seriously lose out at this point if we do not get more able men into the ministry, men who have been educated at colleges and universities and trained in the seminaries. Far too few are preparing for the ministry now. Here at Morehouse College we have 831 students, but only about 20 or 25 so far as we know are looking toward the ministry.

It is my belief that the responsibility for this lack can be laid, at least in part, at the door of the laymen of the church, the congregation itself. If the Baptist laymen will demand educated, trained ministers, they will get them. So long as they put up with untrained men, then our intelligent and gifted young men, even those with a leaning toward the ministry, will not offer themselves for the pastorates of churches where the ministerial standards are low.

Fortunately, there is a change coming, slowly, but coming.

More Negroes are being graduated from high school. More Negroes are being graduated from college, and more are going on to the graduate schools. Such people will not tolerate the preacher who depends on showmanship and emotionalism and who makes no appeal to reason and spiritual conviction. As an indication of what I mean I received a letter just the other day from a church in Detroit asking for a recommendation for a minister. The letter stipulated that the man must have a college degree and a Bachelor of Divinity degree. None other need apply. This advance, you see, was from the laymen. The level of Baptist preaching everywhere will be raised if the laymen of each church will require education and training of its ministers.

I would like to see every Baptist church become a recruiting station to get promising young men committed to the ministry. Medicine is recruiting; law is recruiting; industry is recruiting; government is recruiting. I suppose that some twenty-five governmental and industrial agencies will come here to Morehouse College during the year looking for able people. I think that our churches, too, have got to compete, seeking out leading young men to become Baptist ministers, or we will be left with ordinary men, good fellows but mediocre. But, you say, a man is "called." Maybe he is, but I don't think that we ought to leave all the responsibility to the young men. I think that we should do our part to make it easier for them to accept the call.

I mentioned the character of the preaching of bygone days, the golden streets and the crowns; but there is one thing, for all its unworldly character, that should be said: these preachers *believed* what they preached and nobody wondered if the preacher was really showing his heart. It is difficult for a man to listen to a preacher preach one thing in the pulpit then let his pronouncements die in his word.

Where are the Baptists on this? How far have we come?

Some have come a long way. The freedom of the Baptist churches, the absolute autonomy of each church, is something wonderful and fine; but it is also perilous. In the autonomy of the church a preacher can be shackled by this very freedom of his congregation, and this is a terrible thing. The stand of a church on social issues can be lowered and its spiritual responsibilities smothered by the domination of a few men.

The failure of individual churches in their obvious social obligations is playing its part in the thinking of the young men who might have gone into the ministry and become great leaders among the Baptists. They are saying that they will not be subjected to this domination, and rather than endure it they will forego the ministry and go instead into medicine or law. Others, already in the seminaries, are saying that they will not be silenced in their beliefs. Many are turning away from their home communities and are going to places where they can speak out. Many are going into Christian service other than the ministry. Many are leaving the Baptist churches entirely and are joining other denominations. In time, of course, this will show in the quality of our preachers.

I think that the Baptists face a real loss because there is no doubt but that the Roman Catholic Church is going to remove absolutely every obstacle based on race and class, both in school and church. I think that the Episcopalians are going to follow a close second. The Presbyterians and the Methodists may move more slowly; but the moment they do, they are going to make tremendous inroads, I think, on Negro Baptist membership and possibly on the whites, too. The lack, I think, is in the leadership. Our ministers have not found a way to speak out—though most of them want to—and really be heard. But it is not ministers alone who are responsible for this failure, because again I must say that in some churches small groups of laymen, by no means necessarily representing the majority, have been allowed to take control and dominate the actions of the church.

What can be done about it? There are many laymen who do not agree with the small groups, but they don't tell their ministers how they feel, don't offer their support and promise their backing. They take the time to write their Congressmen to let them know their position on political issues, but they don't speak to their ministers and clarify their stand on church issues.

These difficulties face us particularly in regard to the young people of the congregations. Unless a man can preach the whole Gospel he cannot confront young people. They spot it when he ducks, when he dodges, and they check out. They may leave that church and go to some other church, or to some other denomination where the minister or the priest seems to speak more clearly on the issues that confront them, more directly to their needs and concerns.

It is up to each church to say that *this* church is God's house. Any man in this community who puts his foot on the steps of this church, who walks across its threshold is entering God's house, and God rules here, and God shall decide who enters.

If the Roman Catholic church can say this with its hierarchy then the Baptist church with its freedom ought to be able to say it, freely and gladly within its heart, without the slow and grudging yielding, the piecemeal surrender to the inevitable social and spiritual forces that will triumph, that even now are showing the meaning of God's word, the essence of the Gospel.

Before God and in the presence of Jesus Christ either all men are brothers or no men are brothers. Either God is the Father of all men or He is the Father of none. Either all or none. There is no other way.

# TELL ME THEIR BELIEFS

# *What Makes a Baptist a Baptist?*

Josef Nordenhaug
General Secretary
Baptist World Alliance

In a Baptist church there is a communion table but no altar. There is a Bible on the pulpit because the Baptists hold the Bible to be God's authoritative word for the church and for its individual members. There is usually a baptistry in the church because the Baptists baptize by immersion and the baptistry is needed for this purpose. If there is no baptistry then the people go to the creek or to the shore and the minister lowers the baptismal candidate into the water, taking care that each is completely immersed.

The Baptists observe the Lord's Supper, taking the bread and the cup. They worship God and serve the Lord Jesus Christ without a formal creed or church hierarchy. They hold that the individual soul has direct access to God. They believe that every follower of Christ should be a witness, an evangelist for Christ.

These are interesting facts about the Baptists, and you have heard them often before, perhaps from childhood; but if this were all we knew about Baptists we would know little.

There is so much more to tell, and a Baptist ought to tell his story; just as an Anglican ought to tell the story of his communion, a Methodist the story of his fellow believers, and a Roman Catholic of his church. I doubt, however, that any two Baptists would tell their story exactly alike, for there are many individual convictions and practices among Baptists. This may be due to their stress on individual freedom and liberty of conscience, as well as the fact that each local Baptist church is autonomous. Yet Baptists work together in conventions or unions for common purposes, and enjoy world-wide fellowship in an organization called the Baptist World Alliance. This is all on a voluntary basis. The amazing thing about Baptists is not their differences, although they are many, but the fact that without any central power structure they work together as well as they do.

So I shall try to set forth some basic principles which I believe make a Baptist a Baptist. This matter of what makes a Baptist a Baptist is an intriguing question, but I think that maybe there is a risk in it and I believe that we should make some reservations. If we are going to focus on what is distinctive about us as Baptists, we may give the impression that we look on ourselves as set apart and that we do not have very much in common with others. The truth is that in our beliefs we Baptists have a great deal in common with other Christians: the Fatherhood of God, the Saviorhood and the Lordship of Christ, the presence of the Holy Spirit, the nature and function of the church and its destiny and task and mission. We gladly join with many other church groups in the great basic truths of the Christian religion, while at the same time we retain those attributes that make us distinctly Baptist, believing with all our hearts and all our minds that these attributes are vital to the Christian life.

A very wise Danish philosopher of the last century, Sören

Kierkegaard, said: "Christianity begins with a statement of what the Christian should be, not praise for what he is." So I think it is with the Baptists, and we will here consider certain basic convictions. I know, of course, that a part of what I say will not apply to every Baptist or to every Baptist church, but I don't think that should keep us from seeking to set forth the principles we seek to follow. Just because the climbers don't all reach the top of the mountain there is no reason to doubt that it is there.

So we come back to the question: what makes a Baptist a Baptist? I believe that there are five attributes that a person must have if he is to be a Baptist. And he must have *all* of them. Take one away and he can be something else, perhaps something very fine, but he is not a Baptist.

None of these qualities is a Baptist monopoly and you will find them in many churches and denominations. A person of some other church may say to us: "Why, that is not yours alone. We have that also." Of course they have, but we are not talking about one attribute, or even two or three. We are talking about a combination of five. In my judgment it is *the combination* that characterizes a person as a Baptist.

The first of them is that a person must have a spiritual experience, a personal experience of God. We Baptists have no creed, no catechism, but each person must answer for himself a basic question: Have I had a personal encounter with God? Have I myself come to know Him as the Father, the Creator, the Holy God? Have I been confronted with the Gospel? Do I want to live by its teachings? Have I realized the meaning of Christ for my life? Have I had a spiritual rebirth?

The term we use for this spiritual rebirth is "regeneration," and sometimes, I am afraid, we use it too easily. The term does not signify a gradual development of good qualities, or taking on some new moral habits, or just living "a better life." It means an absolutely radical change that overcomes the old sinful nature of man, which makes him a "new man" now living in the light of a new understanding and faith. This is what being reborn means. It is an experience that a man has, and *knows* that he has had. Through repentance and faith in Christ he comes into a newness of life.

The second attribute of a Baptist is his trust in the Lord Jesus Christ and His undelegated authority. Christ said: "To me is given all authority in heaven and on earth." He never told anybody: "You're going to be my vicar; you're going to act on my behalf. I'm giving you my power of attorney and you go ahead and act for me."

His authority is undelegated and not shared with any human being. He completely retains his own authority in his direct relationship with every person through the Holy Spirit.

As a Baptist I do not believe that certain people are appointed to determine my relationship with God, and I believe that *anything* that comes between God and the human soul is an intrusion. I do not believe it to be God's plan that we should sit outside in some waiting room where an ecclesiastical person sets God's appointments and tells us when he will take us in for an audience. As a Baptist I believe that every man, the humblest of men, has the right through the "once for all" sacrifice of Christ to respond to God for himself, and by God's grace fully to enjoy the presence of God in worship and service.

The third attribute of a Baptist is his *personal faith* in Jesus Christ, and baptism upon profession of this faith.

A man is not born with this faith, nor can it be gained for him by another. In the New Testament you read that those who confessed Christ and professed their faith in Him were added to the church. It was a *community of believers* and each person testified for himself and was taken in on the basis of his own faith. A man can be born into a Christian family or in a country that is called a Christian country, but this does not make him a Christian. Faith is not a collective experience and no man is a Christian by geography or inheritance. Nor is he a Christian by proxy or sponsor or any ecclesiastical manipulation whatever. A man is a Christian only by his own personal faith and his personal commitment to Jesus Christ. This does not minimize the importance of the fellowship of the church or the sacred responsibility of Christian parents.

A personal faith is not private faith. We must make a clear distinction between "personal" and "private." Something that is private a man keeps to himself, but personal faith concerns not only the man himself but all men. A personal faith means a personal obligation to share the Gospel with his neighbors and all men. A believer's faith is personal, but it brims over for others.

After a man has confronted the holy, righteous, and loving God and has accepted God's forgiveness of his sins in Christ, and after he professes his personal faith and his commitment to Christ, he is ready to ask for baptism. Baptists hold that faith comes before baptism, not baptism before faith. A man is baptized only after he has been regenerated by the Spirit of God and has professed faith in Christ, since we believe that there is no regeneration or salvation in the baptismal water itself. I believe baptism is a high and holy symbol, gathering into dramatic focus the believer's passing from the old sinful life into a newness of life, as described in the sixth chapter of Romans: "Therefore we are buried with him by baptism into death: that like as Christ was raised up from the dead by the glory of the Father, even so we also should walk in newness of life." It is our privilege to be baptized; it is our duty to be baptized; and in the pattern of the New Testament immersed in the waters, buried so that we may rise again in the newness of life.

The fourth attribute of a Baptist is his deep respect for the God-given dignity of man. Baptists therefore seek to establish and safeguard full religious liberty—for all men. This liberty implies that all men should be free to follow their conscience in matters of religion, and that political powers or civic law shall not attempt to determine or direct the religious life of citizens.

The dignity of man is a common teaching in all denominations, I suppose, and an element in all democracies; but the Baptists give it the meaning that each individual has the right to deal with God for himself. There can be no greater recognition of the dignity of man than respect for the individual's right of free access to God. This right is a basic conviction of the Baptists. Through the years they have stood for the sanctity and competence of every man, yet they place no man above another. Their continuous teaching is that in the presence of God all men stand equal.

Access to God is not only the ultimate evidence of man's dignity but also the final basis of his freedom, and the freedom of man to worship as he will is a constant objective of the Baptists. They have been, and are now, determined to keep the way clear between the human soul and God.

The Baptists say, and have always said, that the mercy of God and the grace of Jesus Christ are free and open to any man. They have been imprisoned for saying it, publicly whipped for saying it, driven into the wilderness, killed for saying it, and they have gone right on saying it, and they say it now: The mercy of God and the grace of Jesus Christ are free to any man. Knock and it shall be opened. God is always there Himself, waiting for each man to come in. The way is clear. You have access.

All this is voluntary. It is up to you. You can decide. There is the Bible. In it God has given us a sufficient guide for faith and life. The scriptures testify to the Lord Jesus Christ. Read it for yourself. God invites every man to discover the truth of the Bible for himself and to interpret it for himself. But, you say, this may lead to false interpretation. Of course it may. And yet if a man searches before the Lord with an honest heart, the Holy Spirit will teach him. Only as each man listens to the Holy Spirit and has personal faith can he be free in his worship of God and voluntary in his following of Christ.

This freedom the Baptists do not ask for themselves alone. It is their unwavering contention that liberty of conscience and freedom of worship is the true and fundamental right of every human being. Baptists believe that there is no other name than the name of Jesus whereby we must be saved. They do not hold that any religion is as good as the other. They hold Christ to be the incarnate Son of God, but they will not and cannot force anyone to worship God and follow Christ against his will. Each man has the right to worship God as he chooses; or not to worship God, if that is the decision of his mind and the dictate of his spirit. The Baptists demand this basic right of religious liberty for themselves, but they demand it with equal fervor for all men whether they be Protestants, Catholics, Jews, Mohammedans, Hindus, pagans, or infidels. Each man has his own right to profess his faith in his own way, whatever it may be, and to practice his worship, however it may be, so long as it does not interfere with public order and safety and the rights and freedoms of others.

God made man in His own image and gave him freedom. In order to be morally responsible, man must be free. That freedom is not to be violated by any other man, by any church, or by the civic law or the state. The state has no right to order or to deny the worship of any man. It has no right, by the use of human statute, to dictate the form of any man's worship. It has no right to control, or to seek to influence, a man's relationship with God; or to interpose itself in any way between man and God. It shall "make no law respecting an establishment of religion, or prohibiting the free exercise thereof . . ." The state is not equipped to enter a man's conscience and tell him wherein his religion is right or wrong.

As the church and state are separate in organization, in nature, and in purpose, they must remain separate in the administration of their affairs. This is a basic Baptist principle, and its unyielding advocacy by Baptists has played a part in the freedom of this nation and in the sovereign rights of people everywhere. The doctrine of separateness is essential, for when men of political design seek to maneuver or control a church, the spiritual life of the church is threatened; and when a church controls and uses the state for the enforcement of its creeds, then violence is done to the God-given dignity of man.

The fifth attribute of a Baptist is that he accepts the responsibility to bear witness for Christ.

In the practice of full religious freedom a man should not only have the right to believe according to his conscience but he must also have the right to propagate his religion. A follower of Christ has the obligation to put forth the Gospel, to report his conviction and bear public witness.

We Baptists speak of the "priesthood of the believers," a phrase that can be interpreted in several ways but actually means that all who believe in Christ have certain duties given to them which concern others as well as themselves. Every person in relationship with Christ through faith is a witness of Christ to others. This stewardship is a sacred trust, and our witness and intercession are our expression of concern for all men before God.

The Christian religion is not something a man can keep to

himself. If you are a believer you want to tell it and bear witness. If you bear witness publicly you will be heard. And your life and character must back up that witness or else it is false. There is solace in private prayer and our faith can be nurtured in private devotions, but it can flourish only when we share it in public witness of our relationship with God and our faith in Christ as our personal Savior.

These are the five attributes, I believe, that a man needs in combination to make him a Baptist. If he does not have a sense of the sovereign love of God and a personal experience of God, he is no Baptist. If he denies the undelegated authority of Christ and holds that some custodian is in charge of Christ's affairs, he is not a Baptist. If he omits the experience of accepting the Gospel through repentance and personal faith before his baptism and lets some church have faith for him, or his godfather have faith for him, he is not a Baptist. If he overlooks the dignity of man or the voluntary principle in faith, he is not a Baptist. And if he is a non-witnessing man, keeping his religion to himself, he is not a Baptist. Of course, there are many other attributes which enter into the making of a Baptist; but these five, it seems to me, are basic and I would call a man a Baptist on these terms.

Now I feel that there are two other subjects that I should speak about, not that they are the exclusive possession of a Baptist, not that they bestow grace, not that either of them is a vehicle of salvation, but they are a part of our Baptist living and I feel that I should speak of the two ordinances: baptism and the Lord's Supper.

What does baptism mean to me as a Baptist? It means that *after* I hear the word of God and believe, after I repent of any sins and accept the grace of Christ, and after I commit myself to Jesus Christ, I am ready to ask for baptism, and, through baptism, to enter into the fellowship of a church.

Baptism pictures burial of the old life and resurrection with Christ in a new life. The resurrection with Christ is not some mysterious operation of some strange element in baptism itself. The new life cannot be realized except in the living company of Christ. Baptism, for me, is a tremendous and wonderful portrayal of death to sin and resurrection to a life in fellowship with the risen Lord.

Among the Christian groups of today we find several forms of baptism. There is the form of infant baptism which, of course, is precluded by all those who say that hearing the word and believing it must precede baptism. Believing requires a maturity and response which an infant cannot give. Sprinkling is another form which fails to convey the full symbolism of baptism. If baptism pictures a burial and a resurrection then its symbolism is lost in anything less than immersion. In baptism God communicates the highest meaning of life, which is that we must die in ourselves and rise with Him. The form is essential to a symbol. Change the form of baptism and you have marred its symbolism of burial and rising.

I find no sanction for infant baptism in the New Testament. It is a ritual that destroys its own symbolism. But the baptism of believers by immersion conveys to me in striking ways death to sin and the rising to newness of life.

In the Lord's Supper the bread and the wine are symbols of Christ's body and His blood. This commemorates His death and atonement; it is a memorial spoken of in the Gospels and also in the eleventh chapter of First Corinthians: "This do in remembrance of me." This memorial meal reminds us of our dependence in our spiritual life on nourishment by Him.

I could not agree with the theory that the bread and the wine in some mysterious fashion actually become the body and blood of Christ, as is held by some churches. From this I draw back. I believe that Jesus meant simply that we, as his followers, as ordinary human beings, at frequent intervals need a reminder of the great events in the life of Christ and of our essential dependence on Him. Since everybody eats bread and since wine was a common drink in those days, Christ gave to His church this simple symbolic meal as a reminder to remember Him. It brings us face to face with the sacrifice of Christ and we come to the Lord's Supper not to be overawed by some recurring miracle, but to nourish and renew our faith.

# *Inside a Baptist Church*

Theodore F. Adams
Pastor
First Baptist Church
Richmond, Virginia

We drive along a village lane or walk along a city street and there we see a church. This is God's house, a special place, a way of saying we know that God lives in this town. It says, too, that here are men of faith and talent; their faith is chronicled in this stone and wood and glass. They dreamed and gave and worked to make their dream come true. It is their meeting place, a temple they built to the glory of God and a church home where they come to worship. This village or city would be a lonely place without it and others like it. There is something friendly and comforting and blessed as we walk along and see a church.

What goes on inside this building? What happens here? There are sermons and hymns and prayers—this we know. If it is a Baptist church, there are baptisms and the Lord's Supper, with the bread and the cup, and a wide variety of activities. This, too, we know or have heard about. But what else is there inside a Baptist church? Well, in the church where I am a pastor, which is much like all Baptist churches in its ways, there was something the other Sunday morning which you might not see in many churches other than a Baptist church.

More deacons were needed, six of them, and the Chairman of the Nominating Committee stood before the congregation and nominated six men. This was at the morning service, after we had sung our hymns, had prayed, and I had preached the sermon. After the chairman had made the nominations I put the names to a vote by the congregation. The members of the church raised their hands and voted and the deacons were elected.

I asked the new deacons to come forward and read to them the passage from the First Epistle to Timothy, the third chapter: "Likewise must the deacons be grave, not doubletongued, not given to much wine, not greedy of filthy lucre; Holding the mystery of the faith in pure conscience. . . ." After the reading, I said to them: "If you are prepared to accept this high office in this church, will you indicate it by kneeling here before the congregation." They knelt for a prayer of dedication and then they were formally welcomed by the Chairman of the Board of Deacons. After this we gathered at the Lord's Table and observed the Lord's Supper, the deacons assisting in the service. When it was over, the people of the congregation came forward to welcome the new deacons to their office.

I said a moment ago that you might have seen something in this Baptist church on that Sunday morning which is not a common sight in churches. In all churches you see people singing and praying and listening to the pastor's sermon. In some churches you see people kneeling and engaging in various forms of worship, but here in this church the people were electing their deacons by the democratic process of voting, each vote being equal to any other, and the majority deciding. This is the Baptist way of carrying on the Lord's business.

No one could appoint the deacons for this church or for any other Baptist church. No person or group or organization anywhere can lay down the law for any Baptist church. Only the members of each church can decide for themselves. Nor can any one church tell any other church what to do. Two Baptist churches may vote—and they often do—just the opposite from each other, but neither has a say-so in the affairs of the other. Every Baptist church makes its own decisions and each respects the decisions of the others.

But, you ask—and I assure you that you are not the first to ask—how do Baptists with their many churches, each independent and without a central controlling body, continue to function and to accomplish all that they do?

We never speak of *the* Baptist church. There is no such thing. There is no central church, no controlling body, no deciding unit. As a matter of fact, included in what you might call the Baptist denomination, there are many Baptist Associations and Conventions. These are voluntary organizations formed by individual Baptist churches that agree to work together to win the world to Christ.

We can try to sum up this "un-united union" of Baptist churches—and I think that we come pretty close—with the phrase "fellowship of believers" in Jesus Christ as Savior and Lord. Each church is autonomous in the sense that it chooses its own officers and leaders and calls its own pastor. It pays its own way and is an independent unit in the over-all democracy of Baptist churches. We are not bound together by ecclesiastical law or tradition, but we Baptists share very deep and enduring convictions as regenerated and baptized believers, associated by covenant in the faith and fellowship of the Gospel. We are banded together for worship and study and service.

Wherever you find people who have been reading the New Testament you will find people who share common convictions; and there, certainly, will you find Baptists.

At this point I think that we should emphasize one very important fact and clarify it. For all the democracy among the Baptists, and all the independence of each Baptist church, we must clearly understand that there *is* one church, the church universal of the Lord Jesus Christ. This is *the* church, known only to faith because it is constituted in and by the Holy Spirit. Within this church eternal are included our many local churches.

Each of these churches derives its ultimate character not from its membership but from its Head. The controlling principle of government for any local church is the lordship of Jesus Christ. The autonomy of each church rests upon the fact that Christ is present in each congregation and is the Head of each congregation. Autonomy is exercised only under the rule of Jesus; and, therefore, how could any church be subordinate to the rule of any other? How could any church, autonomous under the presence and lordship of Christ, surrender its autonomy to any organization, or group or individual whatever?

Suppose now we go back inside a Baptist church, as we were when we saw the deacons, and this time we look at the pastor. He is no different, in the sense of church membership, from any other member of the congregation. His duties are different from theirs, but what he does should never overshadow the fact that each member of the congregation also has his responsibilities. In fact, in the early life of the church the deacons were known as "servants of the church." Nor has this concept lessened for the deacons, for the pastor, or for any other member of a Baptist church.

In a Baptist church membership has one supreme privilege: the privilege of serving and giving and living for Christ.

In talking about a pastor we sometimes hear the expression "He has had *the call.*" What does this mean? Some people brush it aside as only a "saying." I don't feel that way about it. I think it is very important. I think that it describes a very profound experience with a very deep meaning.

I was sitting on the porch of my father-in-law's house one day talking with a friend. We were talking about the ministry and he said, "You know, Ted, preachers used to be 'called,' but they aren't any more. They just choose their jobs like any other profession." And I wondered what preacher lived or worked or acted in such a way as to make my friend think this, because that is a far cry from our concept of a Christian called to service as a minister.

I believe that every Christian has a vocation, a calling under God. Each man is made in the image of God, with certain talents and abilities, and whatever his daily work he should feel this sense of vocation and know that he is called by God to serve his fellow man in his particular way. I believe, however, that in church-related work there is a special sense of call beyond the influence of any human factor. A man is called in a divine way to the ministry or to missions, to speak for God as the prophets spoke, and to minister as the priests of long ago in the "priesthood of all believers."

When men and women heed this special call to Christian service they open the way to the greatest joys and privileges that life can hold. I remember when I felt called to the ministry. It was as clear to me as any experience in my life, and I have never doubted it since. Nor would I take anything in exchange for the sense of call and its dedication.

While the experience is certain and unmistakable, it does not necessarily come suddenly, as it is commonly supposed to do. Instead, it may be a developing experience and then a realization. I think that it may mean even more when it comes in this way. But however long the development and whatever its course, there ought to be some decisive time at which the individual is conscious that he yields his life to the will of God. When I was a young man looking forward to a life of service we signed a commitment that said: "I will live my life under God for others rather than for myself. I will seek by prayer and study to find God's will for my life, and, when I find it, I will follow it wheresoever it may take me, cost what it may." You don't sign a statement like that without a real sense of call and dedication.

Once a call to the Gospel ministry is clear to a man and he decides to give himself to this service he needs to be trained and ordained. A Baptist minister is usually ordained by the church where he is a member. There are no binding rules governing the procedure of ordination, and any Baptist church, in its full freedom, can ordain anyone it wants. The churches, however, are responsible under God for their actions. In ordination they should maintain high standards as to Christian faith, experience and character, and should be careful about the training of those they ordain, always encouraging young men to seek adequate preparation for their life work in the ministry.

There is a growing feeling among some Baptists that when a man is ordained to the Gospel ministry he is not ordained by the local church alone, in the sense that the church operates entirely independently. Since he will be serving other churches later representatives of other local churches are usually invited to counsel as to whether he should be ordained. An examining council is called, usually through the local Baptist Association, where the man makes a statement and is questioned about his Christian experience, his call to the ministry, and his basic beliefs. When the committee is satisfied, they recommend to the local church that it proceed with the ordination.

We like this procedure of bringing the Association in because it helps to avoid the ordination of unqualified but popular men by local churches. Of course any church is still free to go ahead and ordain any man it pleases, but men ordained without the co-operation of other churches are not always recognized in the larger fellowship. Here in Virginia, for example, each church sends to its Association a list of ordained ministers that belong to its congregations. Each Association, in turn, gives to our state office a list of ordained men in all its churches. This is the official list that is published by the state. It is also the list sent to the Southern Baptist Convention for publication.

At our Richmond church, after we have received a recommendation that a man be ordained, we have a service of ordination. The sermon usually is preached by someone the candidate chooses. He may want the church pastor to preach or one of his seminary professors or some other minister. He is free to invite whomever he wishes.

There is also a charge to the candidate, and if he has already been called to a church as its minister we have a charge to that church. We present the candidate with a Bible, letting him choose the version that will mean the most to him. It is a symbol of our confidence and trust in him as a minister, and of our love for him. It is also an indication that he is to be a preacher of the Word.

The service closes with a prayer of ordination by an ordained minister and a benediction by the candidate. All ordained Baptist ministers present are invited to join with the one who is giving the ordination prayer in laying their hands on the candidate as he kneels. His ordination by the church and the laying on of hands are symbols of the fact that he is not alone in history but is a part of an enduring tradition and of a long line of men who have shared the same privileges.

The laying on of hands carries back to the New Testament custom of setting men apart for special service. Its significance was indicated by Paul when he wrote to Timothy in his first letter: "Lay hands suddenly on no man . . ." The congregation in our church reserves the laying on of hands for men who are ordained to the Gospel ministry. Some churches lay hands on their deacons and ordain them, but we think that there is a little problem here. If you are electing deacons for life you might well ordain them, but if you are electing a man for five years only and he may never serve again what then? Is he still a deacon or isn't he? Some churches say that they have deacons who are in active service and some who are not, but this also makes for complications. Here again, as in other matters, customs differ in different Baptist churches.

We have spoken of the deacons before and we should have some idea of what they do. In some churches they represent the church in all legal matters and in everything pertaining to the ownership and upkeep of church property. Deacons may serve on the Finance Committee or on any other committee. Any one of them may serve as church treasurer, financial secretary, clerk, or in any other general office of the church.

In most churches the deacons participate in both administrative and spiritual matters, and sometimes it is hard to separate one from the other. Whatever else they do, they are concerned with the spiritual life of the church and its evangelistic program. They are concerned with visitation, the care of the poor and needy, and the conduct of the worship services. They counsel with the pastor about the general program of the church, and they often serve as ushers and receive the morning offering, bringing it to the Lord's Table. They act with the pastor in serving the Lord's Supper.

Besides the Board of Deacons, there are, in many Baptist churches, other administrative laymen's organizations, such as the Board of Trustees and the Church Council. In some churches all property is bought and sold in the name of the trustees. They are the recognized legal body of the church, the state looking to them in matters of both property and law. In other churches the trustees are responsible for the entire financial program.

Where there is a Church Council it is usually an over-all body made up of the pastor, the staff, and representatives of various organizations in the church. At its meetings the Council listens to reports from every department and organization. General plans of development are likely to be discussed in the Council before being presented to the church body as a whole. While the Council is representative and originates plans and makes suggestions it usually has no legislative authority or control. That remains with the church.

In many of the large city churches we have come a long way from the time when one man, the pastor, did it all. This would be impossible today. With congregations of thousands, with physical plants extending over most of a city square and including numbers of buildings, and with income and outlay running higher than in many businesses, the modern city church requires not only a dedicated pastor, deacons, and other laymen but also a staff of trained, professional leaders employed by the church and serving full time.

Probably no two churches have exactly the same staff, but, according to its size and needs, a church could employ, besides the pastor, a church secretary or several secretaries, a Minister of Education, Minister of Music, a social worker, business administrator, hostess, supervisor of visitation, student director, counselor, and specialists to work with different age groups—children, young people, and adults. Few, if any, churches would employ all of these people; but whatever number is required, the pastor will act as chief of staff and the others will work in association with him.

Some may feel that the churches are over-organized and look back longingly to the simpler good old days. They liked it better, so they say, when Brother Jones unlocked the church doors on Sunday morning, rang the bell, preached the sermon, and then went home with Deacon Smith to eat fried chicken and hot biscuits. Well, those *were* good old days and the Lord was well served, but now, in the cities at least, things have changed. We just cannot administer a large city church today as Brother Jones handled the limited affairs of his church, any more than we can drive down the main street of Richmond with the same casual abandon that Brother Jones drove his buggy along the sandy road on his way to morning worship.

In considering the ways and the workings of a Baptist church we might mention the matter of church discipline, even though both the subject and the practice are now a little out of date. We don't have as much church discipline as we used to have, say, a century ago. When people were put out of the church then they were sometimes called up before a meeting of the congregation and were questioned and then were formally dismissed. That happens very rarely now. Our discipline is more the kind you find within a family. We call ours a church family, and we try, with the same sort of love and guidance that is used in the home, to lead our people in the way of right and truth and to win them back if they have erred.

Sometimes, though, people disassociate themselves from the family. When this happens to us we are sorry and we recognize the fact that they are gone. In our church we put them on an inactive role because they have made themselves inactive. If we can ever win them back, or the Spirit of the Lord touches them and they come back, then we put them on the active roll again.

A church has the right to dismiss, though, and could exercise that right if it would. In the same way an Association has the right to dismiss a church from its fellowship on questions of theology or on other matters.

A good many years ago the Association in this area—it was not even called the Richmond Association then—wanted to discipline our church because two men in it were in the liquor business. But a very wise man told the Association: "Don't you dismiss the First Church of Richmond or try to coerce it. You let First Church handle its own members." That course was followed by the Association, and eventually the two men got out of the liquor business; but this was done within the church rather than by the Association.

Among Baptist churches, and inside each church, you will find quite a variety of views and convictions. You cannot give a man the right to follow his own conscience, as we Baptists most certainly do, without respecting his right to hold his own views and make his sincere contention for them. To me it is one of our real glories that Baptists can have diversity in thinking and conviction while continuing an underlying unity in Christ.

We differ about theological interpretations and about church practices and customs. We differ in our stands on social issues and on applying the principle of the separation of church and state. Differences of opinion are in the tradition of Baptists, but we maintain communication so that we can talk about these things, possibly reaching an agreement on fact and principle, possibly continuing in disagreement without lessening in love and fellowship.

There is one question at present, a prominent question, on which there is disagreement among some Baptist churches.

It is the question of segregation, in particular segregation as it concerns the churches.

The Baptist World Alliance will not hold a world congress where there would be segregation or discrimination of any kind against any Baptist in the meeting place or in accommodations or food or anything else. This is a basic fact of our fellowship. It is true, however, that these problems and divisions apparently are universal, and wherever you go, into whatever country, you will find a certain measure of separation or segregation or discrimination. Sometimes this is based on nationality; sometimes on color, race, or religion. You will find it in every land in one form or another, and you need only to visit a few other countries to find how true it is.

When you come to our country you find a variety of practices. Some of our Baptist churches will not let members of other races worship with them, just as some of our churches will not let members of other Baptist churches take the Lord's Supper with them. They draw the line very close. Some of our churches will let people of some races worship with them and not people of other races. There is no set pattern.

Here in our church in Richmond anyone is welcome to worship with us who comes to worship God in the name of Christ. I think that more and more churches are coming to this position. In this issue I might not agree with the decisions that some churches have made and might wish that they would make different ones, but I respect their right to follow their own conscientious convictions.

We Baptists reach around the world and include people of every race and color. One of the tragic facts of our time is that the average Christian—young man or woman—knows almost no one of another race who is of comparable education and culture and performance. We need to find ways to help foster understanding and respect.

We not only reach around the world but we go back into history. We Baptists ought to know our past, our record through the years, and the people who suffered and died for their faith—which is our faith too. It is no light thing for the young people of the present to hold this heritage and play their part in a continuing faith. Will they pass it on stronger or weakened? Will it be finer because of them or suffer from their complacency, indifference, and ignorance? To accept and practice the faith we cherish, and to pass it on even stronger and better, is a magnificent responsibility for Baptist young people to recognize and accept.

It is important for young people everywhere to find this faith for themselves and to seek God's will for their lives. It is important that each young person makes the most of his one life, wherever he goes or whatever work he feels led of God to choose. It is no easy thing for a man to make the most of his life and to live for Christ and others rather than only for himself, but as a Christian he can be content with nothing less.

Along with planning and making the most of their own lives young people have the privilege of Christian service, which includes working for others. If young people believe in the right of each individual to make his own choice in matters of religion then they have a constant and unyielding responsibility to see that he has the information and the truth to enable him to make the right choice. This is the basis of our concern for evangelism and missions. This is the faith and the way of life we cherish inside a Baptist church.

It is the way that leads to the salvation of the world, for which we, as followers of Jesus Christ, will work and will pray.

# THERE IS NO END
# TO THE STORY

# There Is No End to the Story

R. Dean Goodwin
Executive Director
Division of Communication
American Baptist Convention

All books end. In a few more pages we will write "The End" to this book. We will put a stop to the writing with two three-letter words, as if you could end an idea, as if you could stop a thought, as if you could take the longings of people and finish them off with two words, The End, and say, "This is it."

It is not! There is more.

A book has to stop somewhere. So much paper, so much ink, so many pages, so many revolutions of the printing press, and then you have to stop and send it to the bindery, where they put a cover on it and wrap it up. Then it is finished, that is, the book is finished.

But you cannot do that with people, with life, with God. The Baptist story is about people and their lives in God; and there is no end to the Baptist story.

Take people's desire for freedom, for instance—"soul liberty" the Baptists called it a long time ago. The idea possessed them. Without such freedom they could eat, buy clothing, have a warm place by the fire in a cosy home, and they could even have friends. Men like John Bunyan and Roger Williams had all this. But for them it was not enough. They wanted freedom. They would go hungry for it; they would freeze in winter storms, sleep in the forests, give up friends, and even life itself. But freedom! They would never give that up.

This love of freedom has not ended. In fact, what has previously happened in the battle for freedom is like firing a firecracker compared to the atomic blast that is the scope of the fight today. It is heard everywhere that people are not entirely free. There is no end to the struggle for freedom.

Nor is there an end to the idea which Baptists have that man cannot be crushed. He is a person! He lives with the conviction that God made him to stand upright and to believe in himself. And so people, *little* people, that the world never heard of before are becoming God's men in the sense that they have never been before. They are determined to stand firm in their self-respect, and unyielding in God's plan for each man to care for every other man.

These are fine ideas and noble convictions, but to end here would be an injustice to the Baptists. The Baptists have never been ready to stop with thoughts, even inspired thoughts. *Acts* grow out of their ideas as simply and as directly as wheat grows from the grain that men plant. Do you believe in the idea that God wants people to go all over the world to preach the Gospel to every person? Then you go yourself as a missionary or you help to send others.

Do you believe that everybody in the Baptist church, the man in the last row at the back of the church as well as the deacon down front and the preacher in the pulpit and the young couple in the balcony—do you believe that all of them ought to be showing everyday examples of just how God lives in people? If you believe this, then you go to school and to work and to play and to the supermarket and, someday, you go to the moon perhaps, but always you act and work like one of God's people. The work of the Christian—which is to live as God's person *really*—started a long time ago. And there is no end to this, either. There will be plenty of such living for you tomorrow and the next day and for as long as you can see ahead and as far into space as you can imagine. It is there before you, before all men. It is endless.

Freedom for the man God created and freedom in the work of responsible people are both old and new experiments in the world laboratory in which we live. Some careless experimenter could blow up the laboratory with the highly explosive stuff of freedom, or some persons who don't have any use for the experiment might halt it for a little while. But if they do, some unknown person, hidden in a remote spot in the universe, will fashion crude instruments and begin the experiment all over again. He will keep at it, too, until that way of life which God wants men to have is here, and fully here, for everyone.

What the Baptists stand for was set in motion by God himself—and surely there is no end to that, not only to the story but to the eternal fact itself. As long as the surf pounds the ocean shores, as long as trees and grasslands turn green in the springtime these ideas and the work that goes with them will point to ever new beginnings in life.

Everyone who enters honestly and deeply into this way of living makes a surprising discovery: that the "best things in life" belong to him whose real satisfaction is in the endless beginning and never in "The End." If what is finished is so easily finished, then we worked for too little. So we end a book, but we do not end the Baptist story. Like life itself the story is full of meaning, and it will go on as we endlessly live it with God, for that is eternal life.

# APPENDIX

# DID YOU KNOW THIS ABOUT THE BAPTISTS?

C. E. Bryant
Director of Publications
Baptist World Alliance

# *How the Baptists Administer Their Affairs*

Autonomy is the distinctive word in any discussion of Baptist organizational structure—or lack of it. The concept doubtless would result in anarchy in any realm outside the spiritual. But Baptists make it work remarkably well.

Insofar as there is an organizational structure with Baptists, it is this:

Local churches
District Associations
State Conventions
National Conventions
Ecumenical groups
Baptist World Alliance

## *CHURCHES*

Baptists speak of the "Church" or "church" in two contexts, and differentiate the two by capitalization of one and non-capitalization of the other.

Church, with the capital c, speaks of the universal Church of Christ encompassing all people of all time who profess faith in Jesus as Savior and claim the name of Christian. This is the great spiritual Church, unlimited by denominational lines or by national or continental boundaries.

For a local congregation "church" is written with a little c. It is, ideally, a group of individuals who look to Christ for guidance, but who, by forming a church, cast their lots together for worship and for ministering in His name.

One speaks of Southern Baptist churches or American Baptist churches, but never of *The* Southern Baptist Church. The distinction accentuates the autonomy of each local church and the authority of each congregation to govern itself without accepting dictation from any higher body.

Each Baptist church calls its own pastor and otherwise handles its own organization and expenditures. It administers its own ordinances: baptism and the Lord's Supper. It determines how it will carry on its program of missions, and in all affairs is its own authority.

## *DISTRICT ASSOCIATIONS*

Churches within a community, a county, or any other limited geographical area sometimes band together for co-operative purposes. These Associations of churches usually call their organizations only by that name—an Association. The organization has no authority over the churches and, in fact, no authority of any kind except as the churches assign responsibility to it.

The Associations provide a means of co-operation wherein churches can promote Bible schools, training programs, women's work, and other phases of local church activity. They usually meet annually or more often for information and planning. An Association can get "experts" as speakers or leaders not available to individual local churches. The Associations work alone, or band together as the churches see fit, to establish youth camps, to conduct mission work within their over-all areas, and to oversee certain benevolences on the community level beyond the financial and personnel abilities of individual churches.

## *STATE CONVENTIONS*

Just as churches of an area join in an Association, so churches in a state co-operate in a State Convention to accomplish missionary, benevolent, and educational goals on a co-operative statewide plan. They jointly employ missionaries and evangelists for remote areas of the state where individual churches cannot extend their individual ministries. They co-operate on a statewide program to establish colleges for the Christian education of young people, hospitals for the care of the sick, homes for homeless children and for the aged.

## *NATIONAL CONVENTIONS*

National Conventions, such as the Southern Baptist Convention and the American Baptist Convention are projections of the State Convention concept. They establish seminaries, publish literature, promote educational programs for the churches, and carry on home and foreign mission programs.

National Conventions, along with State Conventions and Associations, generally consist of messengers appointed by the individual churches. With the missionary Baptists, this representation is based on financial contributions to the work of the Convention. As an example, the charter of the Southern Baptist Convention recognizes one messenger from each church which is in friendly cooperation with the Convention and contributes. Additional messengers are recognized, one for each two hundred fifty members or two hundred fifty dollars contributed, with a limit of ten.

Annual sessions of the Conventions enable representatives of the churches to hear reports and make plans. Always the planning is on a co-operative basis without any vote of the annual meeting or any pronouncement by a convention official considered binding on any church. If an individual church disagrees with the program of its National (or State) Convention it is free not to co-operate in that program.

## *ECUMENICAL GROUPS*

Though the word ecumenical is disliked by many Baptists, because they fear that the merging of denominations might lead to a watering down of doctrine, there is a growing tendency in churches to co-operate beyond their own Convention activities. This co-operation is in local, state, and national Councils of Churches, in which Christian people speak in a united way on social, moral, or political issues, and minister to relief needs where catastrophe strikes.

The Southern Baptist Convention churches have generally stood apart from joining such ecumenical councils, but the American Baptist Convention and several other Baptist groups have joined the National Council of Churches and the World Council of Churches. They see the Council as a way to extend their Christian witness without sacrificing either doctrinal beliefs or autonomy.

## *BAPTIST WORLD ALLIANCE*

Baptists around the world have organized the Baptist World Alliance, which brings together the approximately 25 million members of Baptist churches in 115 countries for "fellowship, service, and cooperation." Its headquarters are in Washington, D.C., from where international communication "helps all the Baptists of all the world to know each other better." Here again the desire is co-operation, and the Alliance has no administrative authority that would conflict with the programs of either local churches or any of their Conventions.

Baptists of the world come together every five years for mass meetings known as Baptist World Congresses. When the Alliance was organized in 1905 in London the assembled Baptists stated the organization's purposes in this preamble to the Constitution:

> The Baptist World Alliance, extending over every part of the world, exists in order more fully to show the essential oneness of Baptist people in the Lord Jesus Christ, to impart inspiration to the brotherhood, and to promote the spirit of fellowship, service, and cooperation among its members; but this Alliance may in no way interfere with the independence of the churches or assume administrative functions of existing organizations.

In the way that I have outlined here, the Baptists carry on their administrative affairs through the various organizations I have named, without there being any central dominant church or any central ruling body of any kind whatever.

# *Some Baptist Terms and What They Mean*

*Alien immersion:* Though Baptist churches generally accept for membership in a local congregation any person who has been baptized into another Baptist church, some churches reject the baptism of churches other than Baptist (therefore, alien), even though the baptism was by immersion. Other Baptist churches make a practice of accepting such new members, provided their baptism was by immersion and meets the definition of believer's baptism.
*Anabaptists:* This term, meaning re-baptizers, was applied to churchmen of Europe, and later in the American Colonies, who rejected infant baptism and insisted on believer's baptism. They therefore baptized a person after his profession of faith even though he had been previously baptized, usually by sprinkling, as an infant.
*Arminianism:* A system of theology propounded by Jacobus Arminius (1560–1609) in protest against the Calvinistic doctrines of irresistible grace and unconditional election. He mag-

nified man's freedom of choice, teaching that although God knows in advance that man will sin of his own free choice, God does not predestine him to do so.

*Atonement:* The act of the sinless Christ's sacrificial death on behalf of, and in the place of, sinful man, so that those who, in faith, depend upon that sacrifice may be made right with God. Thus one can say that the atoning death of Christ brought reconciliation between God and man.

*Baptism:* This word is lifted from the Greek word, *baptizo*, which means to immerse. After a profession of faith a person submits to immersion as a symbol of death to an old life and resurrection into a new life.

*Believer's baptism:* Baptists interpret baptism as evidence of one's faith in Christ. It must therefore come *after* a person believes, *after* a profession of faith or belief.

*Calvinism:* A system of theology propounded by John Calvin (1509–1564), whose basic doctrine is the sovereignty of God. A doctrine of "election" or predestination—meaning that God foresees or predetermines whether a man will or will not be saved—is attributed to Calvin.

*Closed communion:* Some Baptist churches consider the Lord's Supper as an observance restricted to the particular local congregation and do not invite other Christians, even members of other Baptist churches, to participate in the observance. *Open* communion, on the other hand, is the practice exercised by some Baptist churches wherein all Christians are invited to participate in the observance.

*Grace:* A term applied to God's love in action, redeeming men from their sin and sustaining them in a new life in Christ.

*Great Commission:* This reference is to the commission or command given by Christ just prior to his ascension that disciples, or believers, were to spread the Gospel to the ends of the earth. (Matthew 28:19–20)

*Laying on of Hands:* An act, originating in the scriptures (Acts 6:6; 8:17; I Timothy 4:14), whereby ministers and/or deacons symbolize the transfer of spiritual responsibility to a new minister or a new deacon in an ordination service. The ordained men lay their hands on the head of the person being ordained and pray God's blessings on the individual.

*Messenger:* Southern Baptists use this term in lieu of delegate to refer to voting participants in an annual meeting of the district Association or a Convention. A messenger is distinguished from a delegate, as generally defined, in that he is not delegated to speak for the church from which he comes nor can his vote obligate the church from which he comes.

*Ministry:* This term is used primarily to refer to the work of ordained pastors of the churches, both in the pulpit and in the giving of spiritual help to others. It has come to be applied to every area of the church's influence, such as ministry of evangelism, ministry of teaching, ministry of healing, and so forth. In the concept of priesthood of the believers every believer has a responsibility to minister.

*Pedobaptism:* The baptism of infants, a practice rejected by Baptists.

*Priesthood of believers:* Baptists hold that each man is his own priest, directly and personally responsible to God for his decisions and his conduct. This carries with it the idea of responsibility of all believers, laymen as well as clergymen, to bear witness to their faith. The concept is a basic principle of religious liberty, in that a man directly responsible to God should not be restrained in that relationship by any church or governmental authority.

*Regeneration:* The act of being born again to a spiritual life, or the complete spiritual reformation that comes to one's life as a result of repentance and profession of faith.

*Repentance:* The act of a new believer in turning his back on a life of sin and turning his face to a life of faith in God and dedication to obedience of Christ's teachings.

*Salvation:* Man, being born in sin, is doomed to hell or everlasting punishment after physical death, but he can be saved from this lost condition by professing faith in Christ, repenting of his sins, and being sanctified.

*Sanctification:* The process by which a Christian attains moral and spiritual perfection according to the will of God. This process continues throughout life, and results from the presence of the Holy Spirit and continued dedication on the part of the individual.

*Sin:* Any departure or deviation from the divine will of God.

*Soul:* The spiritual element of man. The soul is distinguished from the body in that a body dies but the soul lives forever. The body is thought of as the temple of the soul on earth.

*The Call:* A term specifically used to describe a person's conviction that he should become a minister, missionary, or enter some other specialized Christian vocation. It is generally used to describe any Christian's belief that God has in some special manner indicated His will or desire that the individual serve Him.

*Witness:* A witness in the Christian sense is one who testifies to his faith in Christ. The scriptures quote Christ, "ye shall be witnesses unto me . . ." Believers are encouraged to witness, or testify, of their faith to daily associates, as well as to extend their witness through missionary endeavors.

# *Baptists Around the World*

The Baptists of the world wear saris in India, "Western" clothes in Europe and the Americas, and only scant clothing in the tropical countries. Their faces are of numerous colors and they salute a variety of flags. They speak a thousand languages and dialects. They eat many kinds of food.

Baptists worship in temples of many kinds of architecture: simple assembly halls as well as majestic sanctuaries in the Americas, mud huts in some tropical villages, straw shelters in the jungles.

The warrior of New Guinea destroys his fetishes and thereby proves the sincerity of his profession of faith in Christ as Savior. In other parts of the world a simple walk down a church aisle is sufficient evidence of repentance. Some churches cling to a central pulpit; others prefer the divided chancel. Some Baptists frown on the use of tobacco, others on the use of alcoholic beverages of any kind, others on dancing and card playing. Most of them observe Sunday as their day of worship, but one group, the Seventh-Day Baptists, worship on Saturday.

These differences do not keep any of them from being Baptists, for Baptists are identified by their acceptances of great cardinal truths that bind them in a spiritual fellowship.

Baptists live, worship, and work in 115 different countries. The Gospel story came to most of them through missionaries and migration. But Baptists exist also in countries where missionaries have never gone, Russia for instance.

The first Russian Baptist found his belief by reading a Bible he borrowed from a Greek Orthodox priest. He drew up his own set of doctrine, and then, years later, learned from a traveling German merchant that there were some "people called Baptists" in other parts of the world who held the same beliefs. The evangelistic spirit of that Russian, Nicholai Veronin, who lived in the middle of the last century, has multiplied until there are now 550,000 Russian Baptists. There are more Baptists in the Communist-dominated USSR than in any other country of the world except for the USA.

Here is the Baptist population of the world, reported in September, 1963, by the Baptist World Alliance:

## *AFRICA*

| | |
|---|---|
| Algeria | – |
| Angola | 3,000 |
| Basutoland | – |
| Burundi | 1,509 |
| Cameroon, West | 42,871 |
| Cameroun, East | 13,000 |
| Cape Verde Islands | – |
| Central African Republic | 18,349 |
| Congo Republic | 2,221 |
| Egypt | 164 |
| Ethiopia | 35 |

| | |
|---|---:|
| Ghana | 3,100 |
| Guinea | – |
| Ivory Coast | 1,343 |
| Kenya | 530 |
| Liberia | 14,290 |
| Morocco | 50 |
| Mozambique | 2,250 |
| Nigeria | 62,812 |
| Nyasaland | 2,486 |
| Republic of Chad | – |
| Republic of the Congo | 183,051 |
| Rhodesia, Northern | 2,357 |
| Rhodesia, Southern | 3,183 |
| Rwanda | 1,491 |
| St. Helena | 80 |
| Senegal | – |
| Sierra Leone | 228 |
| South Africa | 43,015 |
| Southwest Africa | 25 |
| Tanganyika | 404 |
| Uganda | – |
| Total for Africa | 401,844 |

*ASIA*

| | |
|---|---:|
| Burma | 212,858 |
| Ceylon | 3,203 |
| China (Mainland) | 123,000 |
| Hong Kong | 18,047 |
| India | 438,868 |
| Japan | 23,703 |
| Korea | 5,210 |
| Macao | 690 |
| Malaya | 1,231 |
| Nepal | – |
| Okinawa | 1,014 |

| | |
|---|---|
| Pakistan | 17,867 |
| Singapore | 886 |
| South Vietnam | 26 |
| Taiwan | 10,000 |
| Thailand | 3,460 |
| Total for Asia | 860,063 |

## *CENTRAL AMERICA*

| | |
|---|---|
| Bahamas | 6,180 |
| Bermuda | 153 |
| British Honduras | 117 |
| Costa Rica | 867 |
| Cuba | 17,888 |
| Dominican Republic | 175 |
| El Salvador | 3,306 |
| French West Indies | – |
| Guatemala | 2,107 |
| Haiti | 41,382 |
| Honduras | 346 |
| Jamaica | 29,496 |
| Nicaragua | 4,182 |
| Panama | 4,476 |
| Puerto Rico | 7,629 |
| St. Lucia | 150 |
| St. Vincent | 150 |
| Trinidad and Tobago | 1,280 |
| Total for Central America | 119,884 |

## *EUROPE*

| | |
|---|---|
| Austria | 750 |
| Belgium | 300 |
| Bulgaria | 700 |
| Czechoslovakia | 4,288 |
| Denmark | 7,196 |
| Finland | 3,321 |

| | |
|---|---|
| France | 2,531 |
| Germany | 96,686 |
| Great Britain and Ireland | 310,437 |
| (Scotland 19,423) | |
| (Wales 89,855) | |
| Greece | – |
| Hungary | 19,600 |
| Italy | 5,000 |
| Netherlands | 8,828 |
| Norway | 6,977 |
| Poland | 2,158 |
| Portugal | 952 |
| Romania | 85,510 |
| Spain | 3,800 |
| Sweden | 30,782 |
| Switzerland | 1,452 |
| USSR | 550,000 |
| (Estonia 9,000) | |
| (Latvia 7,000) | |
| (Lithuania 400) | |
| Yugoslavia | 3,595 |
| Total for Europe | 1,144,863 |

## *MIDDLE EAST*

| | |
|---|---|
| Cyprus | – |
| Gaza | 17 |
| Israel | 138 |
| Jordan | 185 |
| Lebanon | 355 |
| Turkey | – |
| Total for Middle East | 695 |

## *SOUTH AMERICA*

| | |
|---|---|
| Argentina | 15,119 |
| Bolivia | 1,546 |

| | |
|---|---|
| Brazil | 191,692 |
| British Guiana | 279 |
| Chile | 10,000 |
| Colombia | 4,000 |
| Ecuador | 222 |
| Paraguay | 738 |
| Peru | 710 |
| Surinam | 42 |
| Uruguay | 1,135 |
| Venezuela | 1,487 |
| Total for South America | 226,970 |

## *SOUTHWEST PACIFIC*

| | |
|---|---|
| Australia | 40,624 |
| Guam | – |
| Indonesia | 1,979 |
| New Guinea | 4,234 |
| New Zealand | 15,642 |
| Philippines | 28,535 |
| Total for Southwest Pacific | 91,014 |

## *NORTH AMERICA*

| | |
|---|---|
| Canada | 174,863 |
| Mexico | 60,000 |
| United States | 22,151,389 |
| Total for North America | 22,386,253 |
| Grand Total | 25,231,435 |

Baptists are known to be in all countries listed. A blank in the numbers column indicates no figures are currently available.

# *The Baptist Conventions of the United States*

In the United States the Baptists have as many as twenty-nine National conventions. The variations may be due more to geographical, cultural, historical, and even language differences than to differing interpretations of the scriptures. These various Conventions are named below, with a word about each of them.

The statistics about the number of churches and the memberships, which are as up to date as possible, were gathered by the Baptist World Alliance and the National Council of Churches of Christ in the United States.

The four Conventions that are named first include in their membership ninety per cent of all Baptists in the United States.

## *SOUTHERN BAPTIST CONVENTION*

Baptists of the South organized the Southern Baptist Convention at Augusta, Georgia, in 1845. The Convention territory has in recent years spread from the South to all states of the Union.

Churches: 32,598 Membership: 10,193,052

*AMERICAN BAPTIST CONVENTION*

Although missionary organizational developments began in 1814, the Convention was not formed until 1907. Formerly known as the Northern Baptist Convention, this body changed its name to American Baptist Convention at the annual meeting in Boston, 1950.

Churches: 6,276 Membership: 1,559,103

*NATIONAL BAPTIST CONVENTION, USA, INC.*

The older and parent convention of Negro Baptists. It traces its beginning to the organization of the Foreign Mission Convention at Montgomery, Alabama, 1880.

Churches: 26,000 Membership: 5,500,000

*NATIONAL BAPTIST CONVENTION OF AMERICA*

This group of Negro Baptists, ordinarily referred to as the "unincorporated" body, grew out of a 1915 division with the original Convention over operational procedures for the Convention's publishing house at Nashville.

Churches: 11,398 Membership: 2,668,799

*AMERICAN BAPTIST ASSOCIATION*

A Baptist body in the South and Southwest which differed with the Southern Baptist Convention over the primacy of the local church in administration of the ordinances and mission work. The Association was organized at Texarkana, Arkansas, in 1905.

Churches: 3,117 Membership: 650,800

*BAPTIST GENERAL CONFERENCE*

This body was formerly known as the Swedish Baptist General Conference of America; it has operated as a general conference since 1879.

Churches: 545 Membership: 77,200

*BETHEL BAPTIST ASSEMBLY, INC.*

Originally the Evangelistic Ministerial Alliance founded in Evansville, Indiana, 1934.

Churches: 27 Membership: 6,925

*CHRISTIAN UNITY BAPTIST ASSOCIATION*

Organized in 1934, with emphasis on fundamental doctrines, it serves churches primarily in Virginia and North Carolina.

Churches: 12 Membership: 643

*CONSERVATIVE BAPTIST ASSOCIATION OF AMERICA*

This group of churches withdrew from the Northern Baptist Convention in protest against allegedly liberal tendencies in organization and doctrine. Organized May 17, 1947, Atlantic City, New Jersey.

Churches: 1,351 Membership: 300,000

*DUCK RIVER (AND KINDRED) ASSOCIATIONS OF BAPTISTS*

A group of Baptist Associations found in the Duck River area of Tennessee, Alabama, Georgia, and Mississippi.

Churches: 28 Membership: 3,141

*FREE WILL BAPTISTS*

This is a body of Arminian Baptists (named for James Arminius of Holland) organized in the South in 1727 by Paul Palmer and in the North in 1787 by Benjamin Randall. It embraces churches in thirty-four states and in certain other countries. The organization in the United States is known as the National Association of Free Will Baptists.

Churches: 2,150 Membership: 193,664

*GENERAL CONFERENCE OF THE EVANGELICAL BAPTIST CHURCH, INC.*

Organized among independent Free Will Baptist Churches in 1935, it is in fellowship with several Free Will Baptist Conferences. Was formerly known as the Church of the Full Gospel, Inc.

Churches: 31 Membership: 2,200 (1952)

*THE GENERAL ASSOCIATION OF REGULAR BAPTIST CHURCHES*

Founded in May, 1932, in Chicago, Illinois, by a group of churches which had withdrawn from the Northern Baptist Convention because of doctrinal differences, places emphasis on the New Hampshire Confession of Faith, with a "premillennial" ending.

Churches: 992 Membership: 143,782

*GENERAL BAPTISTS*

An Arminian (see Free Will) group of Baptists first organized by John Smyth and Thomas Helwys in England, 1607. Transplanted to the colonies in 1714, it died out along the seaboard, but revived in the Midwest in 1823.

Churches: 779 Membership: 58,943

*GENERAL SIX-PRINCIPLE BAPTISTS*

A Baptist group, organized in Rhode Island in 1653, drawing its name from Hebrew 6:1–2 (repentance, faith, baptism, laying on of hands, resurrection, and eternal judgment).

Churches: 4 Membership: 258

*INDEPENDENT BAPTIST CHURCH OF AMERICA*

A body of Swedish Free Baptists, dating back to 1893.

Churches: 2 Membership: 70

*NATIONAL BAPTIST EVANGELICAL LIFE AND SOUL SAVING ASSEMBLY OF USA*

Organized in 1921 by A. A. Banks of Detroit, Michigan, as a charitable, educational, and evangelical organization.

Churches: 264 Membership: 57,674 (1951)

*NATIONAL PRIMITIVE BAPTIST CONVENTION OF THE USA (FORMERLY COLORED PRIMITIVE BAPTISTS)*

A group of Negro Baptists opposed to money-based mission boards and other organizations (see Primitive Baptists). Organized at Huntsville, Alabama, 1907.

Churches: 1,125 Membership: 85,983

*NORTH AMERICAN BAPTIST ASSOCIATION*

Organized May, 1950, in Little Rock, Arkansas, as the result of a division within the ranks of the American Baptist Association.

Churches: 1,980 Membership: 330,265

*NORTH AMERICAN BAPTIST GENERAL CONFERENCE*

These churches emanate from German Baptist immigrants of more than a century ago, the earliest being organized in 1843. Some of them are still bilingual in their ministry.

Churches: 325 Membership: 52,625

*PRIMITIVE BAPTISTS*

A large groups of Baptists, mainly through the South of the United States, who are opposed to organizations, such as

Sunday Schools, and to modern missionary societies. Some churches practice foot washing (John 13:5). They are Calvinistic, placing emphasis on the sovereignty of God.

Churches: 1,000 Membership: 72,000 (as of 1950)

## *PROGRESSIVE BAPTIST CONVENTION OF AMERICA, INC.*

A group of Negro Baptist churches which withdrew from the National Baptist Convention of the USA, Inc., and formed their own organization at Cincinnati, Ohio, in 1961.

Churches: 654 Membership: Unknown

## *REGULAR BAPTISTS*

A group of Baptists in the South of the United States, holding doctrinal positions between Arminianism and the Calvinism of the Primitive Baptists. There are about twenty-two Associations with no general organization.

Churches: 266 Membership: 17,186 (as of 1936)

## *SEPARATE BAPTISTS IN CHRIST*

A group of Baptists found in Indiana, Kentucky, Tennessee, and Illinois, dating back to an Association formed in 1758 in North Carolina. The name comes from those early Baptists who separated themselves from state churches.

Churches: 85 Membership: 7,358

## *THE UNITED FREE WILL BAPTIST CHURCH*

A group of Negro Free Will Churches (see Free Will Baptists) which set up its organization in 1870.

Churches: 836 Membership: 100,000 (as of 1952)

## *SEVENTH-DAY BAPTIST GENERAL CONFERENCE*

A group of Baptists organized in Rhode Island in 1671; they

are distinguished from other groups by their observance of Saturday as the Sabbath.

Churches: 61 Membership: 5,726

*SEVENTH-DAY BAPTISTS (GERMAN, 1728)*

Refugees from the Palatinate, Germany, so-called German Baptist Brethren or Dunkers (because they immersed three times in the name of the Trinity), arrived in Philadelphia in 1720. Some of them observed the seventh day as the Sabbath and organized this body in 1728.

Churches: 3 Membership: 150 (as of 1951)

*TWO-SEED-IN-THE-SPIRIT PREDESTINARIAN BAPTISTS*

Organized in the United States in the latter part of the eighteenth century in protest against Arminian doctrine and in keeping with a conviction that two seeds entered the life stream of humanity in the Garden of Eden, a good seed planted by God and an evil seed planted by the devil. Every child is predestined, born with one seed or the other, and nothing can be done to change his destiny.

Churches: 16 Membership: 201 (as of 1945)

*UNITED BAPTISTS*

This group dates from meetings of Regular Baptists and Separate Baptists, held in Richmond, Virginia, in 1787. There are sixteen Associations in Kentucky, thirty Associations in all. Southern Baptists came largely from this union, dropping the United from their name.

Churches: 568 Membership: 63,641

Total churches 91,839
Total membership 22,151,389

## *BAPTIST COLLEGES, SEMINARIES, HOSPITALS, HOMES FOR CHILDREN, AND HOMES FOR THE AGED IN THE UNITED STATES*

(These figures are close to accurate, though, of course, they will change.)

| | |
|---|---|
| Seminaries | 16 |
| Senior colleges | 61 |
| Junior colleges | 23 |
| Academies | 13 |
| Bible schools | 5 |
| Hospitals | 51 |
| Homes for aged | 72 |
| Children's homes | 40 |

# *Some Books About Baptists*

## *BAPTIST BELIEFS*

*A Baptist Treasury* compiled by Sydnor Stealey: Crowell. An anthology of Baptist thought and contributions to world culture through the centuries.

*Christian Doctrine* by W. T. Conner: Broadman. With keen insight and fresh, clear language, this long-time theology teacher sets forth basic doctrines of the scriptures.

*Fundamentals of Our Faith* by Herschel H. Hobbs: Broadman. What do Baptists believe and why do they believe as they do? This book by a well-known pastor and former president of the Southern Baptist Convention answers these questions clearly and completely.

*A Baptist Manual of Polity and Practice* by Norman H. Maring and Winthrop S. Hudson: Judson. An up-to-date appraisal of Baptists: who they are, what they believe, and how they work together, written by two eminent denominational historians.

## *HISTORY*

*The Baptists* by Frank S. Mead: Broadman. Fire, persecution, and the Baptist surge of freedom pack drama into every page of this stimulating book.

*A History of the Baptists* by Robert G. Torbet: Judson. One of the most thorough and comprehensive books on denominational history, it surveys the origins of Baptist development, particularly in Great Britain and America, and in Europe. Answers a multitude of questions on beliefs and practices and portrays Baptists' role in the drama of human events.

*Baptist Confessions of Faith* by W. L. Lumpkin: Judson. Every important Baptist confession of faith since the seventeenth century is given in full in the light of its historical setting. An indispensable reference book.

*The Southern Baptist Convention: 1845–1953* by W. W. Barnes: Broadman. A recounting of the beginnings, the struggles of wartime, the tensions of dispute, and the realization of what once seemed far-fetched dreams.

*Encyclopedia of Southern Baptists: Broadman.* A thorough and comprehensive coverage of Southern Baptist history, organization, and theological outlook. Articles are included on all State Conventions, Districts, Associations, Convention boards and agencies, state papers, colleges—everything that is Southern Baptist. (Two volumes, 1,544 pages)

*Baptist World Fellowship* by F. Townley Lord: Broadman. A history of the Baptist World Alliance (1905–1955).

*Baptist World Congress Report Books:* Baptist World Alliance. A volume each on world Baptist meetings at Atlanta, 1939; Copenhagen, 1947; Cleveland, 1950; London, 1955; Rio de Janeiro, 1960.

## BAPTISTS AT WORK

*The Baptist Way of Life* by Brooks Hays and John Steely: Prentice-Hall. A layman and a theologian discuss the Baptist heritage, the Baptist concept of Christian service, and Baptist contributions to the world.

*The Baptist Witness* by Henry K. Rowe, revised by Robert G. Torbet: Judson. Discusses the place of Baptists among the Protestant denominations, the ways they worship, biographies of their leaders, their background and heritage of democracy.

*Venture of Faith* by Robert G. Torbet: Judson. A vivid tale of sacrifice, struggle, and achievement. Encompasses the whole history of American Baptist missions. Warm, human.

## *BIOGRAPHY*

*Bill Wallace of China* by Jesse C. Fletcher: Broadman. This book is more than a biography; it is the unfolding of a Southern Baptist medical missionary's selfless life. Dr. Wallace died in a Communist jail after having stayed on in China to continue the work of Stout Memorial Hospital in Wuchow during World War II.

*Champions of Religious Freedom* by Davis C. Woolley: Convention Press. Sets forth principles of religious freedom and gives biographical information about Baptists and others who have championed these principles.

*Billy Graham* by Stanley High: Walfred. A close-up look at this Baptist evangelist who has preached to more people face to face than any other man in history.

*I Found God in Soviet Russia* by John Noble and Glenn D. Everett: St. Martin's Press. When John Noble escaped from a Russian Communist prison, he brought with him a shocking and inspiring eye-witness account of life behind barbed wire. The book details Russian Baptists' struggles to maintain their faith in the face of Communist atheism.

*Tales of Baptist Daring* by Benjamin P. Browne: Judson. These concise biographies show the insight, faith, courage, and dreams of our Baptist ancestors who have paved the way for freedoms that we take for granted.

*Why I Am a Baptist* by Louie D. Newton: Nelson. More

than a glowing biography, this book talks about various kinds of Baptists and recounts many of their contemporary activities.

*To the Golden Shore* by Courtney Anderson: Doubleday (Paper). A fascinating and thorough biography of Adoniram Judson and his missionary activities in Burma. Judson was the first Baptist missionary from North America; he sailed in 1811.